371.02
HUG

ITEM NO: 1904373

1904373

KU-346-201

Closing the Learning Gap

UNIVERSITY OF WALES, NEWPORT
LIBRARY
AND
INFORMATION
SERVICES
CAERLEON

157-167
p82.

Mike Hughes

First Published by
Network Educational Press Ltd
PO Box 635
Stafford ST16 1BF
www.networkpress.co.uk

Published in the USA by
Crown House Publishing Ltd
PO Box 2223, Williston, VT 05495-2223
www.CHPUS.com

First published 1999
First Reprint 2000
Second Reprint 2003
© Mike Hughes 1999

ISBN 1 85539 051 5
Library of Congress Control Number: 2003104526

The right of Mike Hughes to be identified as the author of this work has
been asserted in accordance with Sections 77 and 78 of the Copyright,
Designs and Patents Act 1988.

All rights reserved. No part of this publication may be reproduced, stored in a
retrieval system or reproduced or transmitted in any form or by any other means,
electronic, mechanical, photocopying, recording or otherwise without the prior
written permission of the Publisher. This book may not be lent, resold, hired out
or otherwise disposed of by way of trade in any form of binding or cover other
than that in which it is published, without the prior consent of the Publisher.

Every effort has been made to contact copyright holders and the
Publishers apologize for any omissions, which they will be pleased to rectify
at the earliest opportunity.

Series Editor – Tim Brighouse
Edited by Gina Walker
Design & layout by
Neil Hawkins, Network Educational Press Ltd
Cover & additional illustrations by
Barking Dog Art, Stroud, Glos.

Printed in Great Britain by
MPG Books Ltd, Bodmin, Cornwall

Acknowledgements

I am grateful to all those people who have helped and encouraged
me to write this book. In particular, I wish to thank:

all the teachers and pupils I have had the pleasure of working
with over the last 15 years; they have inspired me to
ask the questions and seek the answers

all those people who are pushing back the boundaries of our
understanding of how the human brain works, and how we learn

the Lakers School 'Learning to Learn' group for their advice and feedback

Barbara Hinton for her help with the original manuscript and
Gina Walker for the improvements she made at the editing stage

Rachel, Ben and Sam for their endless patience and understanding.

Mike Hughes
May, 1999

Foreword

A teacher's task is much more ambitious than it used to be and demands a focus on the subtleties of teaching and learning and on the emerging knowledge of school improvement.

This is what this series is about.

Teaching can be a very lonely activity. The time honoured practice of a single teacher working alone in the classroom is still the norm; yet to operate alone is, in the end, to become isolated and impoverished. This series addresses two issues – the need to focus on practical and useful ideas connected with teaching and learning and the wish thereby to provide some sort of an antidote to the loneliness of the long distance teacher who is daily berated by an anxious society.

Teachers flourish best when, in Key Stage teams or departments (or more rarely whole schools), their talk is predominantly about teaching and learning and where, unconnected with appraisal, they are privileged to observe each other teach; to plan and review their work together; and to practise the habit of learning from each other new teaching techniques. But how does this state of affairs arise? Is it to do with the way staffrooms are physically organized so that the walls bear testimony to interesting articles and in the corner there is a dedicated computer tuned to 'conferences' about SEN, school improvement, the teaching of English and so on, and whether, in consequence, the teacher leaning over the shoulder of the enthusiastic IT colleague sees the promise of interesting practice elsewhere? Has the primary school cracked it when it organizes successive staff meetings in different classrooms and invites the 'host' teacher to start the meeting with a 15 minute exposition of their classroom organization and management? Or is it the same staff sharing, on a rota basis, a slot on successive staff meeting agenda when each in turn reviews a new book they have used with their class? And what of the whole school which now uses 'active' and 'passive' concerts of carefully chosen music as part of their accelerated learning techniques?

It is of course well understood that even excellent teachers feel threatened when first they are observed – hence the epidemic of trauma associated with OFSTED. The constant observation of the teacher in training seems like that of the learner driver. Once you have passed your test and can drive unaccompanied, you do. You often make lots of mistakes and sometimes get into bad habits. Woe betide, however, the back seat driver who tells you so. In the same way the new teacher quickly loses the habit of observing others and being observed. So how do we get a confident, mutual observation debate going? One school I know found a simple and therefore brilliant solution. The Head of the History Department asked that a young colleague plan lessons for her – the Head of Department – to teach. This lesson she then taught, and was observed by the young colleague. There was subsequent discussion, in which the young teacher asked,

> *"Why did you divert the question and answer session I had planned?"*

and was answered by,

> *"Because I could see that I needed to arrest the attention of the group by the window with some 'hands-on' role play, etc."*

This lasted an hour and led to a once-a-term repeat discussion which, in the end, was adopted by the whole school. The whole school subsequently changed the pattern of its meetings to consolidate extended debate about teaching and learning. The two teachers claimed that because one planned and the other taught both were implicated but neither alone was responsible or felt 'got at'.

So there are practices which are both practical and more likely to make teaching a rewarding and successful activity. They can, as it were, increase the likelihood of a teacher surprising the pupils into understanding or doing something they did not think they could do rather than simply entertaining them or, worse still, occupying them. There are ways of helping teachers judge the best method of getting pupil expectation just ahead of self-esteem.

This series focuses on straightforward interventions which individual schools and teachers use to make life more rewarding for themselves and those they teach. Teachers deserve nothing less, for they are the architects of tomorrow's society, and society's ambition for what they achieve increases as each year passes.

Professor Tim Brighouse

Contents

The approach and strategies outlined in this book:

- are designed to encourage teachers to think about classroom practice and, in particular, learning

- will generate debate and discussion about the learning process

- are not independent of each other, nor are they strictly sequential – observing others, for example, often encourages teachers to reflect on their own performance

- should be adapted to suit specific circumstances

- should not be reviewed as one-off activities – they are part of an on-going process.

Introduction

What is the Learning Gap?

Fascination and frustration have prompted me to write this book: fascination in the complexities and enormous potential of the human brain, and frustration that so many of the dramatic and recent breakthroughs in our understanding of the learning process have failed to make a substantial impact on classroom practice.

The 'Learning Gap' is the difference between what we know about effective learning and what is currently happening in the classroom: a difference that should, I believe, underpin the school improvement agenda. It is teachers in the classroom who make the major difference to student achievement and it is therefore teachers, rather than schools, that should be the focus of attention in the drive to raise standards.

Closing the Learning Gap has been written by a teacher, for teachers, and has been deliberately presented in a style that will encourage teachers to spend ten minutes of their lunch hour reading it. Not only have the relatively recent discoveries of how the brain operates and learns been simplified, but particular emphasis has also been placed upon how teachers can apply these messages in their classrooms. This is a book that is grounded in reality and permeated by practical suggestions for developing the quality of teaching in schools.

Consideration is also given to the ways in which teachers with whole-school responsibility for developing the quality of teaching might go about what is undoubtedly a daunting and demanding task. An approach based upon the identification and subsequent closing of the Learning Gap at a variety of levels, ranging from individual teacher to whole school, is outlined. It is an approach that is currently being used in schools all over the country, with great success.

Closing the Learning Gap aims to:

1   encourage teachers to reflect upon the ways in which they teach
2   help teachers, departments and schools to identify and close their Learning Gaps
3   help teachers to apply the recent messages from brain science in their classrooms.

All of the strategies that are outlined are being used in a range of secondary schools, where they have been proved to be effective and successful.

Above all, it is hoped that *Closing the Learning Gap* will stimulate thought and generate discussion about the most important thing we do as teachers – teach lessons.

If the most significant influence upon student attainment is the teacher, then the key to genuine and lasting school improvement must be developing the quality of teaching.

TEACHING IS THE KEY INFLUENCE UPON STUDENT ACHIEVEMENT

> *'Good teaching is the key to high standards of achievement.'*
>
> OFSTED 1998

On the day that last year's GCSE results were published, I bumped into a member of staff who was having some difficulty suppressing both her obvious delight and a quite enormous grin. I was a little puzzled, as the overall results for the school were slightly lower than expected, with results in her department being particularly disappointing. She explained that her delight was for the grades achieved by the children in her own teaching group, and she confessed that she hadn't yet bothered to find out the results for the rest of the department, never mind the rest of the school. She went on to explain how much effort she had put in to helping her students achieve such high grades and how she now felt that it had all been worthwhile.

The incident has stuck in my mind and illustrates for me the importance of the teacher in helping children to achieve in the classroom. This teacher had little or no influence over children's attainment in other areas of the school, but she had gone to extraordinary lengths to ensure that they would succeed in her subject. As their teacher, hers was, by some considerable distance, the most significant influence on the levels of attainment of those students, the influence of any whole-school policies or strategic improvement plans paling into insignificance by comparison.

This book is based on the premise that, if the most significant influence upon student attainment is the teacher, then *the key to genuine and lasting school improvement must be developing the quality of teaching.*

There has been much concern in recent years about underachieving schools, and considerable debate about the extent to which differences in attainment measured in examination success can be attributed to the effectiveness of the school. Many would argue that all schools operate in a unique context and that variations in the quality of the intake, as indicated by prior attainment and the huge differences in levels of parental support, render many comparisons invalid.

Of much greater significance and infinitely greater concern, however, is the variation of achievement within the same school. As data analysis becomes more sophisticated, it is becoming ever more apparent that particular teachers and departments are consistently achieving significantly higher results – even allowing for the relative difficulties of different subjects – while working in the same context and with the same students. Differences such as these are almost always due to variations in the quality of teaching.

'School effectiveness research has shown that teachers and the learning level are three to four times more powerful than the school level.'

Professor David Reynolds

In recent years, many schools have achieved significant improvements in attainment, based upon examination success. Often this has been due to a combination of factors including the provision of extra revision classes, introduction of formal reward systems for high attainment, tightening of procedures for handing in coursework, review of grouping policies, change of examination syllabus, and so on.

These steps are effective, immediate and easy to introduce. However, they are relatively superficial and will only raise achievement so far, with the initial significant improvement in results quickly beginning to plateau. From this point onwards, continued improvement will *only* occur if the quality of learning taking place in the classroom improves.

Improving the quality of the teaching that students experience on a daily basis is, of course, significantly harder to achieve and will not yield dividends anywhere near as dramatically or as quickly. It is, however, the only way to sustain improvement in attainment after the 'quick fix' solutions have been taken.

DEVELOPING THE QUALITY OF TEACHING

If we are confident that long-lasting, genuine school improvement is only achieved by improving the quality of teaching, then teacher improvement has to be our priority. It all sounds so straightforward and yet, as anyone who has experience of trying to develop effective classroom practice will confirm, it is far from simple. Many schools have tried to raise the quality of teaching, only to find that while the good teachers get better, those who desperately need to improve remain relatively untouched by the process.

The feedback that I have received from a wide range of teachers and managers during the last decade suggests that there are two key barriers to the widespread development of high quality teaching:

1 *the difficulties in finding time* for teachers to observe each other teaching – good practice within an institution is rarely widely disseminated

2 *the perceived threat and implied criticism* that existing practice must be somehow inadequate and ineffective – when people feel they are being attacked their natural reaction is to defend.

In many ways these factors are related. The isolation that teachers often enjoy (or at least experience) from the time they rip up their metaphorical 'L plates' to the day they pick up their gold clock, exacerbates feelings of suspicion and significantly contributes to their reluctance to subscribe to a process that might find them wanting.

If these are indeed the factors that are responsible for holding back the development of effective classroom practice, then any attempt to develop the quality of teaching in a school must be careful to take them into account.

The two key barriers to the widespread development of teaching are:

- lack of time
- the perceived threat and implied criticism that existing practice must be somehow inadequate and ineffective.

Therefore, any attempt to develop the quality of teaching must:

- be a priority – this means a considerable commitment of time and financial resources
- minimise the sense of threat.

As Tim Brighouse points out in the foreword, teachers have a lot in common with drivers with neither species taking kindly to back seat advice. Suggesting to a teacher with 20 years experience that they might like to consider ways in which they could make their lessons more effective is akin to suggesting to an experienced driver that they could improve their driving, and is highly likely to meet with the same response!

Creating a climate in which reflection on the quality of teaching, and the sharing of effective practice, is the norm involves a major cultural shift. It does not happen by chance, nor does it take place overnight. Two factors are crucial to its success:

1   *It has to be made a priority.* This means it requires a considerable commitment of time and therefore financial resources. As with any priority, the involvement and leadership of the headteacher is vital.

2   *The sense of threat has to be withdrawn, or at least minimized.* Depersonalize the process: we are looking at the relative effectiveness of strategies, activities and approaches, not people.

The approach to improved classroom practice that is described in this book has been developed over the last ten years, and takes these two key factors very much into account. Its evolution has been guided and heavily influenced by the responses of many teachers from a wide variety of schools, resulting in a strategy that is both effective and practical.

Although it is an approach that has been employed in many schools and departments, it by no means guarantees overnight success. For there are no magic solutions; no course, book or school improvement package that once attended, read or purchased will provide a dramatic short-cut to improved classroom practice. It is inevitably a slow process, with the very teachers who would most benefit from reflecting upon their practice invariably the least enthusiastic to do so. It is time consuming and therefore expensive, although the expense can be viewed as an investment that will ultimately yield enhanced performance and higher standards of attainment.

It is also a journey that will never end, because, no matter how effective a teacher, department or school, they can always improve. Improvements may be more dramatic when starting from a low base, and inevitably there will come a point when highly effective teachers require only fine tuning as opposed to a major overhaul, but we must ensure that all teachers operate within a framework of continuous improvement. OFSTED takes the view that schools should be *excellent or improving or both* – why not teachers?

The Learning Gap:

The difference between what we know about effective learning and what goes on in your classroom.

The Challenge:

Close the gap!

THE LEARNING GAP

The Learning Gap is the difference between what we know about effective learning and what is currently happening in the classroom.

Identifying the Learning Gap, and implementing strategies to close it, is the key to improving the quality of teaching in a school and therefore lies at the very heart of school improvement. In effect, it is the school improvement agenda.

The Learning Gap is highly personal and will vary significantly between individual teachers, faculties and schools. Each teacher will have a Learning Gap and it is highly likely that the size and nature of the gap will be different when teaching top set Year 8 on Tuesday morning to that when teaching bottom set Year 10 on Friday afternoon.

Closing the gap

There are three steps to closing the Learning Gap, which provide the structure for the remainder of this book:

1   Establish what effective learning 'looks like'. Agree on *the goal*.

2   Determine where you are. What is currently happening in your classroom? *The difference between 1 and 2 is your Learning Gap.*

3   Identify and implement strategies to close the gap.

These three steps should not be viewed as one-off activities that once completed need never be revisited. *They are part of an ongoing process* and components of a development loop. Each time strategies are identified and implemented, it is important to review what is the new state of affairs in your classroom and the extent to which you have closed the Learning Gap. This review will, in turn, help you identify future strategies to further close the gap.

There are three key processes that will enable teachers, faculties and schools to establish their Learning Gaps:

1   *Self-reflection*: The perceived threat that invariably accompanies any attempt to develop the quality of teaching is significantly reduced if teachers are encouraged to simply reflect upon their own practice. They are not put in a position of having to reveal their thoughts unless they wish to and this reassurance can make teachers more willing to consider the issue of effective learning. It's a bit like looking in a mirror: you don't have to tell anybody else what you see!

2   *Observation*: Teachers' perceptions of their own practice can often differ from reality, sometimes considerably. Systematic and effective observation by other teachers can complement, enhance and inform the process of self-reflection. Done well – and there is a training implication here – it can be of enormous benefit to both the observer and the observed.

3   *Feedback*: Observation alone is relatively worthless. It is the information gleaned during the observation that is important, and therefore it is the feedback given that is of real value. The fact that few teachers have been trained in this area is short sighted: insensitive feedback can be demoralizing and can quickly persuade teachers to opt out of the improvement process.

Three key processes that will help teachers establish their Learning Gap:

- **self-reflection**

- **observation**

- **feedback.**

These three processes are neither mutually exclusive, nor strictly sequential. It is hard – almost impossible – to observe a colleague without reflecting upon your own practice. Similarly, the very fact that you are being observed sharpens your own awareness of what is happening during the lesson and encourages you to reflect upon your own performance.

I once tried to feed back to a colleague that I had observed, but before I could speak, he proceeded to tell me exactly what had happened during the lesson, identified the strengths and weaknesses and told me how he proposed to amend the lesson the next time! Whether he would have done so to the same extent if he was not being observed, is doubtful.

Many schools are beginning to provide more opportunities for teachers to observe colleagues in action in the classroom. While this is to be applauded, a key message of this book is that simply 'watching' in isolation is relatively worthless. For observation to be effective, not to mention cost-effective, the observer needs to know *exactly* what he or she is looking for.

Having observed a lesson, a colleague once sought me out to tell me how good it had been. He had clearly been impressed and used adjectives such as 'fantastic' and 'superb' to describe it. However, when I asked him *why* he felt the lesson had been so good, he was unable to answer! He had seen a highly effective lesson but the fact that he didn't know why it was good made it extremely unlikely that he would be able to incorporate any of the good practice he had seen into his own teaching.

Observation is an important part of the process of developing the quality of teaching, *but it is only a part*. Teachers must have a clear understanding of the learning process before they can go and look for it in the classroom, and before they can provide effective feedback to other teachers they have observed.

95 per cent of our understanding of how the brain learns has come in the last ten years.

When were you trained?

Section One

Establishing the goal

> *This section deals with the first step in determining the Learning Gap, which involves building up a picture of effective learning and identifying precisely what we are trying to achieve in the classroom.*
>
> *There are two parts to this section:*
> - ☛ *Part one looks at what we know about learning.*
> - ☛ *Part two helps teachers and faculties establish a clear picture of effective learning in their subject. This is their goal.*

PART ONE: WHAT DO WE KNOW ABOUT LEARNING?

We know more about the working of the human brain and understand more about the learning process than ever before and yet, all too often, these important and exciting messages fail to have any impact upon classroom practice. It is a source of considerable frustration and a waste of the dramatic advances in human knowledge that, as a profession and as a society, we can ill afford. It would be interesting to speculate how people would react if advances in medical science were neglected in such a way!

Among the many reasons why the recent advances in brain science have, to date, had relatively little impact in schools, two stand out:

1 *Not all teachers have heard the message.* Sheer volume of work, time pressure and fatigue factor are significant barriers to the dissemination of new information among teachers. The fact that so many of the burdens imposed on the profession have precious little to do with learning is not without irony.

   The task for school managers is to *ensure that teachers have heard and fully understood the message.* At a simple level, this involves creating time for teachers to be able to reflect regularly and consider the learning process. A rather more demanding task is to create the culture that encourages teachers to listen.

2 *Teachers have heard the message but are unsure how to apply it in the classroom.* One colleague that I worked with recently remarked at the end of an INSET session, 'That's all very interesting, but what does it mean for me in my Lab?'

   It is not sufficient that teachers have heard the message. We must also ensure that teachers are able to interpret it so that they can apply it in their classrooms. *Theory has to become practice.*

Asking teachers to place everything they know about learning in rank order is a useful exercise:

- It generates thought and discussion about learning.

- Teachers are encouraged to identify 'learning priorities'.

- The 'threat factor' is reduced as teachers are talking about learning, and not about their own classroom or teaching methods.

- Teachers are encouraged to reflect upon their own practice.

Overleaf are listed ten interesting and significant pieces of information about the learning process. They have been deliberately simplified and written in a style that will, hopefully, encourage teachers to read them. This list then forms the structure for the first part of this section, which not only forms information about the learning process, but also attempts to consider the implications of each piece of information upon classroom practice.

The overall aims of this part of Section One are to provide information, encourage reflection and generate thought and discussion about how students learn. There are many ways of using the information that follows: the approach described below is simply one suggestion. It is suitable for an INSET session involving either a subject team or a group of teachers from different departments.

Using information about learning

- Ask yourselves the question, 'What do I already know about learning?'

- Working individually, write down on a postcard anything you know about the learning process.

- Add all these extra ideas to the *'Ten interesting things about learning'* overleaf. You could copy each idea on to card and laminate them.

- As a team, you are now challenged to rank each point in order of importance.

- Make sure that each point is fully understood. (The *'Ten interesting things'* are each explained in detail in the remainder of this part of Section One.)

- Many teachers will find it hard to 'rank order' all the points. Some groups may wish to set the cards out in a pattern: for example, the three most important points, followed by the five next most important points, and so on.

- There is, of course, no right answer to this exercise and it is of little consequence if teachers fail to complete the rank ordering exercise. *It is the process that is significant.*

As you read through the first part of this section and consider each point in turn, consider two questions:

■ How do I take this into account during my lessons?

■ How could I take this into account during my lessons?

Ten interesting things about learning

1 The brain has an amazing capacity to learn. We use around 2 per cent of our brainpower – this means we waste 98 per cent!

2 The brain needs fuel! Oxygen, water, protein and rest are required for the brain to function efficiently.

3 People do not learn effectively when placed under negative stress – low stress, high challenge is the ideal state for learning.

4 The maximum time for which children can concentrate is approximately two minutes in excess of their chronological age in minutes. Even adults cannot concentrate for longer than 20–25 minutes.

5 People learn more at the beginning and end of a learning experience than they do in the middle. This is sometimes referred to as the BEM principle.

6 People learn in different ways: some will prefer to *see* information (visual learners), some will learn more effectively if they *hear* information (auditory learners) while others will learn best by *doing* – touching, feeling, making (kinesthetic learners).

7 Learning is greatly enhanced when the whole brain is engaged.

8 People remember dramatic, emotional, unexpected experiences. People remember *context* much better than they remember *content*.

9 Recall is dramatically improved when information is regularly reviewed. Without review, information is forgotten almost immediately.

10 People learn best when they *want* to learn. Motivation is therefore very important to effective learning.

'It's a bit like having a tin of beans but no tin opener. What a waste!'

Year 10 student

1   The brain is amazing!

Recent developments in our understanding of the brain demonstrate that up to now we have grossly underestimated our brainpower. The human brain has a staggering capacity to learn that is, in effect, limitless. It is said that there are more possible neural connections within each individual brain than known atoms in the universe, and, although numbers of this magnitude are difficult to comprehend, clearly that is a lot!

Among experts, estimates of the proportion of our brainpower that we actually use vary between 1 per cent and 5 per cent but, whatever the actual figure, the staggering fact remains that each one of us fails to use around 95 per cent of our brain's capacity – what a waste!

Implications for learning
We are significantly underestimating the learning potential of each and every student. Many of the messages and strategies in this book aim to help teachers utilize more of the brainpower of each student they teach. There are many other excellent books on whole-brain or accelerated learning included in the list of suggested further reading on page 183.

You may like to reflect on the following question, but postpone answering it until after you have completed reading the book. As your understanding of how people learn develops, so you will wish to develop your answer.

How can I help students learn more effectively by exploiting more of the enormous capacity of the brain?

- ■ **How could you, as a classroom teacher, help students' brains get the fuel they need?**

- ■ **How could you, as a school, help students' brains get the fuel they need?**

2   The brain needs fuel

The brain uses in excess of 20 per cent of the body's oxygen. It also requires water, rest and protein to function efficiently.

When students sit down, their heart rates slow and the amount of oxygen that gets to their brains decreases by as much as 15 per cent. While students are sitting, often for up to an hour, their brains are becoming increasingly inefficient. Simply standing up and moving around can increase the amount of oxygen getting to the brain, and so improve learning. Similarly, as the morning progresses, children who have not eaten or had a drink since breakfast will find learning more and more difficult as, like a car, they gradually run out of fuel. The problem is significantly worse for children who do not eat a proper breakfast.

Implications for learning
Consider for how much time children sit down during your lessons. Are there any ways in which you can create opportunities for children to stand up and move around the room? This is particularly important if you are teaching a double lesson.

Deliberately leaving a pile of books on the front desk so that students have to leave their seats and collect them is one way of making sure that everyone has to stand up and move around at some time during the lesson. Similarly, it may be that children are required to break into groups or go and collect equipment. An alternative is to let students in on the 'secret' and simply ask them to stand. I once observed a mock examination, which comprised two papers: after Paper One had been collected, every candidate stood up and shook their arms around before they proceeded with Paper Two!

Understandably, teachers are often wary of strategies that involve students leaving their seats in case they become disruptive. Managed skilfully, however, this exercise can have just the opposite effect and enhance learning at the same time.

Just being aware of the situation helps. It may be that schools can increase awareness among students by making sure they *know* that their brains require fuel. I recently taught a group of children I had never previously met as part of a cross-curricular day when the school's normal timetable was suspended. At the end of the day I asked each student to write down the most significant thing that they had learned. One replied, 'Bananas help you learn – I'm going to have them for breakfast.'

At a school level, the provision of drinking fountains or breakfast clubs, and careful reflection on the lengths of lessons and the structure of the school day, are all possible ways of responding to the needs of the brain and making learning more effective.

There is a massive difference between challenge and stress, but only a very thin dividing line; the problem for the teacher is that each child will draw it in a different place.

3   Low stress – high challenge

The human brain is not really designed for 'learning' – certainly not the formal kind of learning that goes on in school classrooms. It is designed for survival. When people feel threatened or are placed under any kind of negative stress, the survival instincts of the brain automatically take over and the chances of any effective learning taking place are just about nil. There is nothing that the individual can do to stop the survival instinct dominating. It is quite natural, and it places the onus very much on the teacher to create a non-threatening learning environment in which the learning brain has a chance to operate.

People learn best when they are at ease and feel comfortable with their surroundings, but are also switched on and ready to learn. This state, often referred to as *'relaxed alertness'*, is the condition we must strive to create if learning is going to be effective. It involves a fine balance and is by no means easy to achieve in a school environment but it is even more unlikely that we will create it if we are not consciously striving for it. Being clear about the atmosphere that we are trying to create must be the starting point.

Not only do people learn best when they feel at ease, they also respond to a *challenge*. Providing challenge is an effective strategy for all students, but it is particularly noticeable how well boys respond to being challenged. At a time when we are all concerned with the relative underachievement of boys, this is a strategy that should not be ignored. *There is a massive difference between challenge and stress, but only a very thin dividing line: the problem for the teacher is that each child will draw it in a different place.*

Implications for learning
Consciously strive to create a learning environment that puts students at their ease. Think carefully about the furniture, layout and wall displays, and the messages they send out as children enter the room. Consider also the way in which you greet students and address them during the lesson. It is believed that over 50 per cent of communication is done non-verbally and, in many respects, it is the manner and mood of the teacher that sets the tone and has a huge bearing upon whether or not learning will be effective.

Start each lesson with a smile. If you can, make eye contact with every student as they enter the room so that they notice your mood and expression. Smiles are replicated and reflected and go a long way to putting people at ease. They send out important messages: 'it's safe in here, come on in, we're going to enjoy this.'

Think carefully too about the way in which you begin your lessons. Many begin with the teacher asking questions, often to recap on the previous lesson. Frequently, questions are directed at individual students since experience tells us that 'question and answer sessions' can easily be dominated by the same few children. However, there are few things less certain to induce stress and prevent the student thinking clearly than being put on the spot like this at the outset!

Create a high challenge learning environment:

- ■ 'I bet you can't think of three reasons...'

- ■ 'Completing this in ten minutes will be a challenge, but I know you're good enough – let's go for it!'

- ■ 'Last time you got six out of ten, now let's see you get at least eight.'

- ■ 'I bet you can't think of more examples than me.'

- ■ 'I bet you can't ask me a really hard question – so hard that I can't answer – at the end of this lesson.'

Provide challenges to individuals, pairs and small groups – watch them respond!

Another major source of stress is the feeling of not being in control. It is a common feeling in many classrooms where students have no responsibility for what they are going to learn, how they are going to learn it or even where they are going to sit! Giving students back some control over learning – *what, how, where* and *when* – is an effective strategy in reducing stress and so enhancing learning.

The feeling of having some control over their learning is best achieved by providing students with some *choice* in the classroom. It need not be difficult to introduce choice into your lessons, yet to do so – by means of a subtle change in emphasis and a handful of simple strategies – can bring about a significant and extremely beneficial change in atmosphere. For example, the teacher, having decided that there should be a test on a recent topic, could ask students:

- Would you prefer to do test A or test B?
- Would you like to do the test at the beginning or end of the lesson?
- You can either write a short paragraph or draw a labelled diagram.
- How would you like to explain this? In writing? By a picture? You choose.

Although the students are given some choice over their learning, it is the teacher who is very much in control of the lesson. There is no question that there is going to be a test, but the provision, or at least the perception, of choice ensures that students respond significantly more positively – they have to make a positive choice, such as A or B – than they would if the teacher had introduced the lesson with, 'Right, we're going to do a test today.'

Thoughtful use of language and a small adjustment in the way activities are introduced and presented can lead to a significant reduction in student stress levels. For example, few things leads to stress quite like the word *test*, particularly if it is accompanied with the promise that anyone who fails to achieve at least seven out of ten will have the pleasure of redoing it!

Consider the ways in which students would respond to these statements. Which would lead to the most/least stress? Which would lead to the best results?

1 Today you're going to have a test.

2 Today I'm going to give you an opportunity to show me how much you know and understand about this topic. Would you like to do that in the first or second half of the lesson?

3 How would you like to show me how much you know and understand about this topic? Would you like to tell me? Show me? Write about it? Draw me a diagram? You decide.

Reflect upon your own lessons:

■ How long do you think your introductions normally last?

■ How would your students answer the question above?

■ How long does your introduction really last? (Many teachers talk, particularly at the beginning of the lesson, for longer than they think!)

■ How many learning activities do you include in a typical lesson?

■ How long do tasks typically last in your lessons?

■ Do you consciously plan your lessons around the students' concentration spans?

■ Do you give students a mental break during lessons?

4 People have limited concentration spans

The average concentration span is limited to approximately chronological age in mintues plus two minutes. The concentration span of an adult is around 20–25 minutes.

This is the reason why even the most conscientious students begin to drift after the teacher has been talking for more than half an hour and the reason why teachers begin to fidget in their seats during INSET sessions. When teachers lose concentration during INSET, they begin to daydream, doodle and look out of the window, but *when children lose concentration many will misbehave and become increasingly disruptive*. If the teacher is still talking 40 minutes after the lesson has started then he or she shouldn't be the least bit surprised if no one is listening!

Implications for learning

Children in Year 7 have a concentration span of less than 15 minutes, while Year 11 students can concentrate for no more than 20 minutes. Teachers must keep this firmly in mind when planning lessons, rather than talking for 40 minutes and bemoaning the fact that students have become inattentive.

Learning is more effective when lessons are divided up into a series of activities. Hour-long lessons certainly require more than one task – they demand at least three – otherwise students will lose concentration. By varying the activities, there is a significantly greater chance that all students – visual, auditory and kinesthetic learners – will have an opportunity to spend at least part of the lesson working in their preferred learning style (see page 41).

A *two-minute break*, or 'time-out', can be a useful way of giving students a mental rest as they approach the end of their natural concentration span. During this period students have an opportunity to reflect on the work they have been doing, talk to a neighbour about it, talk to the teacher, or switch off completely.

Equally significantly, a 'time-out' is an opportunity for the brain to subconsciously file material away and begin to make sense of the information that it has just received. Students 'return' from this brief break from organized learning, particularly if they have had an opportunity to stand up and move around, mentally refreshed and ready for the next challenge.

Collecting and/or giving out homework between learning activities is an alternative way of punctuating a lesson. Frequently, homework is dealt with at the beginning and end of lessons. Spending time collecting homework at the beginning of a lesson, when concentration and anticipation are greatest, is a waste of prime learning time (see page 37). Dealing with homework during the lesson provides a natural break for the students without giving them the unwanted message that the lesson has ended.

The BEM principle

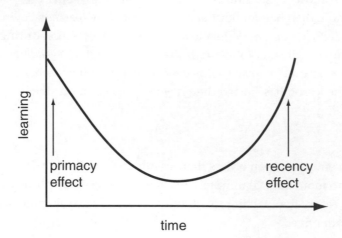

People remember more from the beginning and end of a learning experience than they do from the middle.

These are known as the primacy and recency effects.

Exploiting the BEM principle

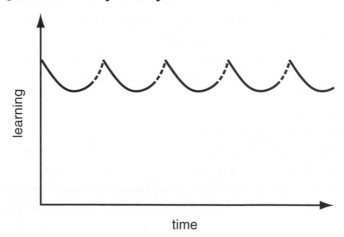

Create lots of 'beginnings' in your lessons to maximize memory and learning.

5   People learn more at the beginning of a learning experience

Students learn more at the beginning and end of a learning experience than they do in the middle. This is sometimes called the BEM (Beginning End Middle) principle.

The beginning, in particular, is the time when the potential for learning is at its greatest, when the relatively high levels of concentration, but particularly *anticipation*, make the learner more receptive. This feeling of anticipation is significantly accentuated by the novelty value generated when the opening activity is different and largely unexpected. It is the optimum time for learning and an opportunity that all teachers would do well to recognize and exploit.

This optimum period for learning does not last for long, however, and as the beginning of a learning experience passes into the middle, so the advantageous conditions created as students embark on an activity quickly wear off.

Implications for learning

Not only should teachers be aware of the BEM principle, they should exploit it and consciously incorporate it into their planning. In particular, consideration should be given to three major classroom implications:

1   *Make the most of the beginning of the lesson.*
    Ironically, the beginning of the lesson is often wasted. Too often, prime learning time is spent collecting homework and giving out resources. Instead, exploit the curiosity that students bring to lessons ('What are we doing today, Miss?') by engaging the class from the first minute. Making the opening dramatic and unusual not only enhances concentration and prolongs the anticipation generated by the start of a lesson, it significantly increases the chances that material will be remembered.

    Although all students are more receptive at the beginning of a learning experience, it is often boys in particular who benefit from a crisp, purposeful start to lessons.

2   *Lessons should have lots of 'beginnings', and be based on a number of activities.*
    Many lessons are based around only one learning activity. This means that there is only one beginning, lots of middle and long periods of time when children are at their least receptive.

    Not only do multi-activity lessons maintain interest and generate their own pace, they continually recreate the feelings of anticipation and heightened concentration associated with the start of an activity, and so improve learning.

    The impact of a multi-activity lesson is particularly acute when the activities themselves are very different. Not only does it keep the students guessing and interested, it ensures that the needs and interests of children with various preferred learning styles (see page 41) are being met.

Reflect upon your own lessons:

■ How do you typically start your lessons?

■ Do you consciously exploit the optimum learning time at the beginning of a lesson?

■ When do you tend to introduce the 'key learning point' of the lesson – is it nearer the beginning or the middle?

■ Do you consciously create lots of 'beginnings' in your lessons?

■ How many activities do you incorporate in a typical lesson?

■ Do you vary the nature of the activities within a lesson?

■ Do you include activities that are different and unexpected?

3   *The most effective time to introduce the key learning point is at the beginning of a learning activity.*

By 'key learning point', I mean 'the bit they *must* all know' – the key piece of the jigsaw, the law or piece of information that is central to the whole topic. Often, students need to understand the key learning point before they can make further progress.

Considerable thought must be given to when the key learning point of the lesson is introduced, with the middle of an activity consciously avoided. Get into the habit of identifying the key point of your lessons and starting with it. Try to introduce it in the first 60 seconds, or at least within five minutes. Make it the first thing you say – even before, 'Good morning'. If you do it consistently, students will soon get the message.

Lessons that start with an introduction by the teacher and a recap on last lesson, typically involving a question and answer session, are in danger of delivering the key message between 25 and 40 minutes after the start. Not only is this the midpoint of the lesson and the exact time when the students are at their least receptive, it is also after the natural concentration span of secondary school students has ended. In short, *the most important bit of many lessons often comes at precisely the worst time!*

To summarize, exploit the BEM principle by:

☞ **making the most of the beginning of the lesson**

☞ **introducing the 'key learning point' at the beginning of the lesson**

☞ **creating lots of 'beginnings' in your lessons.**

During any given class activity, it is safe to assume that approximately two-thirds of the children are working outside their preferred learning style.

6   People learn in different ways

Individuals have different preferred learning styles or, put simply, people learn in different ways.

Some people prefer to see information (visual learners), some will prefer to hear information (auditory learners), while others will learn best by doing – touching, feeling, making (kinesthetic learners). Visual learners can be subdivided into those who prefer to see text and those who learn best from diagrams and pictures.

In a typical secondary school class there will be approximately the same number of children in each of the three categories: one-third will be visual learners, one-third will be auditory learners and one-third will be kinesthetic learners.

These learning styles are *preferences* and do not mean that individuals can only learn in one way. Auditory learners, for example, can learn by looking at information but they *prefer* to hear it. In general terms, however, people learn most effectively when working in their preferred styles.

Although most people can adapt and learn outside their preferred style, there are a few people who will only learn anything of substance in their favoured mode and it is almost certain that these people will be kinesthetic learners. If these students are not given opportunities to work in their preferred learning style, not only will they fail to learn effectively, they could well become disaffected and misbehave. Think of a student who does relatively little in your lessons other than fidget, appears to show no interest and makes very little progress: there is a very good chance that he or she is a kinesthetic learner.

Kinesthetic learners are the students who are most disadvantaged in secondary schools, simply because so many learning activities are based upon reading, writing and listening. This is partly because most teachers, who themselves have been successful in the reading, writing, listening world of formal schooling, are visual or auditory learners and predominantly teach in their preferred style. *All teachers have a preferred style*, which, deliberately or not, is the way in which they predominately operate in the classroom. Even teachers who consciously and successfully vary their style, to cater for the various student preferences, will often slip back into the mode that comes naturally to them when they are under pressure.

Kinesthetic learners generally find that opportunities to work in their preferred style significantly decrease as they get older. There is often a substantial amount of learning during the primary school years that is physical, tactile and generally appealing to the kinesthetic learner. However, as children move into secondary schools, their experiences in the classroom become increasingly visual, while those that make it all the way along the obstacle course into higher education will have to contend with more auditory learning than they have previously encountered.

Visual learners:

- say things like, 'I see' and 'That looks good to me'
- tend to look upwards
- speak rapidly
- like to write, visualize, draw images.

visual mode

Auditory learners:

- say things like, 'That rings a bell' and 'I hear what you're saying'
- tend to have level eye movement
- like to hear a presentation, explain something to someone.

auditory mode

Kinesthetic learners:

- say things like, 'That touched a nerve' and 'I don't follow'
- tend to look down
- fidget, need regular breaks
- like to make things
- walk around when they read.

kinesthetic mode

Closing the Learning Gap

Implications for learning

Teachers should be aware that in every class they teach there are individuals who both prefer to learn, and learn most effectively, in significantly different ways. During any given class activity, it is safe to assume that approximately two-thirds of the children are working outside their preferred styles! Although most students will still be learning, it will be highly unlikely that they will be enjoying themselves as much as they might, and working outside their preferred styles on a regular basis can have a detrimental effect upon their motivation.

It is not necessary to systematically determine each child's preferred style and teach them exclusively in that manner, although some schools are beginning to experiment along these lines. However, it can be worthwhile to know which children belong to each group and in particular to know who the kinesthetic learners are, especially if they are exclusively kinesthetic learners.

There are a wide range of questionnaires available, some written in 'student language', to determine an individual's learning preference, and some teachers and schools are beginning to employ these. However, it is usually possible to identify an individual's preferred style simply by observing him or her and noting the activities in which he or she shows a particular interest and makes progress. A simple checklist of the key characteristics of the various learning groups is provided opposite.

The key, however, to ensuring that all students have opportunities to learn and make progress, is to *employ a wide variety of activities*, to cater for visual, auditory and kinesthetic learners. Ideally, teachers should endeavour to give opportunities to different types of learners by providing a variety of activities *within each lesson*. The need for lessons to include a number of activities in order to create many 'beginnings' has already been established (see page 37). By making sure that these activities are very different in nature, all children, regardless of preferred learning style, have an opportunity to participate and learn. However, when it is not possible to include activities for all three types of learner in every lesson, care must be taken to ensure that there is sufficient variety of activities during a unit or module of work, so that all students have a chance to learn and make progress.

Are you aware of your preferred teaching style?

How do you cater for students with different learning styles in your lessons?

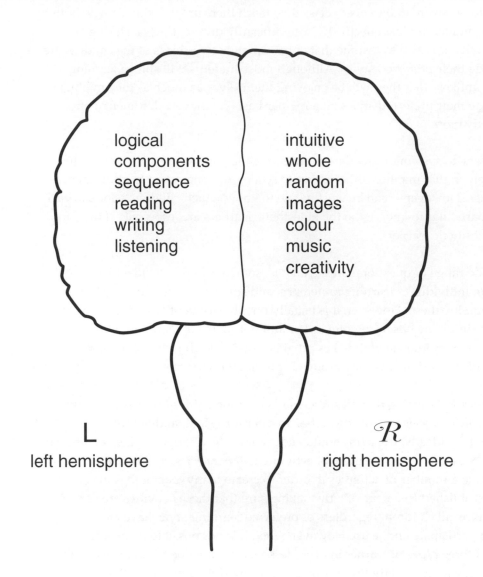

logical | intuitive
components | whole
sequence | random
reading | images
writing | colour
listening | music
 | creativity

L
left hemisphere

R
right hemisphere

We now know that both sides of the brain are involved, to some extent, in virtually all learning activities.

7   Learning is greatly enhanced when the whole brain is engaged

The most recent research tells us that, although the neo-cortex (the 'thinking bit' of the brain) is divided into left and right hemispheres, initial theories that the separate hemispheres perform very different functions were both exaggerated and simplistic. We now know that *both* sides of the brain are involved, to a greater or lesser extent, in virtually *all* activities.

The two hemispheres do, however, operate in very different ways: the left brain processes information logically, dealing effectively with the component parts and preferring to deal with information sequentially; the right brain, meanwhile, prefers to see things as a whole and is comfortable working randomly and intuitively. The left brain also deals with reading, writing and listening, with the right brain responding to pictures, colour and music.

Even this separation of function is very much a generalization. The interconnectivity of the brain is clearly illustrated by the fact that, although it is the left brain that processes the individual words heard when someone speaks to you, it is the rightbrain that responds to the way it is said and interprets the tone, inflection and rhythm. Although in recent years there has been a tendency to encourage 'right-brain' learning, this in many ways has been a desire to compensate for the traditional dominance of 'left-brain activities' in many classrooms. *Both sides of the brain are important in the learning process* and as such our goal should be to *connect the hemispheres* rather than to emphasize one at the expense of the other.

Understanding that the brain is an incredibly complex organ, which thrives when it is receiving and processing information from a variety of sources, gives us some important clues in maximizing learning in the classroom. Not only is the brain able to cope with multisensory simultaneous input, it actually prefers it! Indeed, information that has been received, processed and stored in a variety of ways, is much more likely to be retrieved when it is needed.

Implications for learning
Students spend much of their time during lessons reading, listening and writing. These are very much left-brain activities, which means that the right hemisphere of the brain is often under-used. These activities also tend to favour girls, for whom, in general, the left hemisphere operates at a quicker rate than for boys.

We each have a preferred or dominant hemisphere, the majority of teachers being 'left-brained, analytical thinkers'. As teachers often teach in their preferred style, there may well be a number of students in any class who are disadvantaged because they are predominately 'right-brained thinkers'. Bored high achievers and students with apparent learning difficulties often fall into this category.

It is important, therefore, not only that teachers are aware of this situation, but that they employ a range of strategies during their lessons to engage both sides of the brain in the learning process. *Care must also be taken not to over compensate* – the brain needs left hemisphere activities too. The aim must be to provide a variety of activities to ensure that both sides of the brain are fully activated and that the two hemispheres are connected. This need not be too onerous a challenge, nor does it necessarily mean that teachers have to spend a long time preparing lessons. Simply being aware of the situation and seeking to provide a variety of activities is a step in the right direction.

To connect the hemispheres and enhance learning, ask students to:

- describe (left) a picture or diagram (right)

- visualize (right) a written description (left)

- convert text (left) into a picture (right)

- turn keywords (left) into a poem (right)

- identify key words (left) and write them in a different colour (right).

Show the jigsaw box first

The right hemisphere processes the whole picture (the picture on the front of the jigsaw box) while the left hemisphere processes the component parts (the individual jigsaw pieces). Not surprisingly, the brain finds it easier to complete the task if it sees the whole picture before it concentrates on the smaller pieces and fine detail. This is sometimes referred to as seeing the Big Picture first. Make a conscious effort to provide students with an overview of the topic and an outline of the lesson at the beginning of a learning experience, before going on to provide the detail. Remember: show them the box before they do the jigsaw!

Saturate the brain

Make sure that your classroom is a stimulating environment and that children are working with a range of resources every lesson. The use of posters, wall displays, music, pictures and artefacts to complement books and written material will ensure that both hemispheres are being activated and that the brain is simultaneously receiving information from a range of sources via more than one of the senses. These are the conditions that the brain prefers and in which it will flourish.

Connect the hemispheres

A student who is looking at a graph is primarily using her right brain. By simply asking her to describe the patterns made by the graph, either in writing or orally, the left brain is activated, the hemispheres are connected and learning is enhanced. Too often students work with a resource and are required to do very little with it other than reproduce it. Not only do activities such as these lack challenge and make it extremely difficult to assess the student's understanding, we are limiting learning by activating the hemispheres in isolation.

How much time do students spend on 'left-brain activities' during your lessons?

Do you consciously endeavour to engage and connect both sides of the brain?

'There is now increasing evidence that our memories may not only be far better than we ever thought, but may in fact be perfect.'

Tony Buzan

8   People remember context much better than they remember content

The human brain is not designed for remembering large amounts of information (*content*) and yet this is precisely what children are required to do during the majority of lessons!

Learning content in this way often involves repetition and learning by rote: for the brain this is both unnatural and strictly limited and, without regular rehearsal, the information will only be remembered for a short period. Learning in this way is also heavily dependent upon the motivation of the individual student and this, as any teacher knows, is highly variable.

What the brain does remember well, however, is *context*. This is the reason why students remember well how a waterfall is formed once they have stood in the cold and wet sketching one on a geography field trip. It is also why the entire class can recall what a Victorian classroom looks like after sitting in one, dressed in Victorian clothes, during a visit to a museum.

The brain remembers context quite naturally and has an unlimited capacity for memories such as these. The brain is also proficient at remembering anything that is *emotional, unusual, exaggerated or dramatic*.

Research tells us that many different areas of the brain are used for the purpose of remembering, and that using these so called 'multiple memory systems' is the most powerful way of ensuring that something is remembered. Put simply, this means that the more ways that the brain receives information, the more ways in which it is stored and the more likely it is to be recalled.

Implications for learning
There are two key principles for ensuring that material covered in a lesson is remembered:

1   *Firstly, reduce the amount of rote-based learning that is heavily dependent upon 'content memory' and increase the number of opportunities for students to use their more natural 'context memory'.*

   This does not necessarily require you to arrange a field trip every lesson – although educational visits can be particularly effective – but it does mean that students must be fully *engaged* in the learning experience. The more they are required to *do* – dissect a sheep's heart, role play ordering a drink from a French café, or make a fossil out of Plaster of Paris – the more chance they will remember.

   Actively involving students in their learning greatly increases the chances that they will be using more than one sense, so making recall more likely. Creating a context that engages more than one sense, ideally all five, in every learning experience should be a conscious aim in every lesson.

   Lessons that fail to fully engage the student, and involve copying notes, drawing diagrams and low level comprehension exercises, will be unlikely to be remembered simply because they fail to activate the brain's contextual and multiple memory systems.

Reflect upon your own lessons:

- How much of your lessons do your students remember?

- What proportion of learning in your lessons is 'content' based?

- How many opportunities do you provide for students to learn 'in context'?

- To what extent do you actively engage students? What are they required to do?

- Do you consciously aim to involve all five senses in your lessons?

- If students were asked to predict what activities they would be doing in your next lesson, would they be able to?

- Do you consciously make learning experiences exaggerated and dramatic?

- Do you consciously use unusual and unexpected strategies in your lessons?

- Do you employ 'memory tricks' such as acrostics or mnemonics?

2   *Secondly, make the learning experience as dramatic, emotional and unexpected as possible, as these are the experiences that the brain remembers quite naturally.*

If you can cover material in an unusual way, the novelty value will greatly enhance the chances of it being remembered. This is a factor worth bearing in mind if you are about to introduce a concept or information that is of particular significance in your subject, or a key component of an examination course. When lessons become predictable and are delivered in a dull, matter-of-fact manner, the brain begins to switch off and the chances of information being retained significantly decrease.

It is, of course, extremely difficult to always teach in a dramatic and unusual way. Even teachers who are 'different', are often predictably so. It is therefore important that maximum use is made of the 'novelty factor', by making sure that particularly significant concepts or pieces of information are covered in such a way as to grab the students' attention. Key learning points should be identified as such on all schemes of work and considerable thought given to how these are taught. Build time into your planning sessions and meetings for teachers to share ideas for unusual ways to deliver key information.

The use of 'memory tricks', such as acrostics, rhymes and mnemonics, can also be an effective strategy to improve memory. Such devices can be particularly useful when students are required by the National Curriculum or an examination syllabus to remember key facts and important information, despite the fact that their brains are not designed to do so. The brain remembers best the exaggerated and the unusual and this should be reflected by the acrostic or the mnemonic. Memory 'tricks' are most effective when they are personal, grossly exaggerated and dependent upon the imagination to the extent that they border on the absurd.

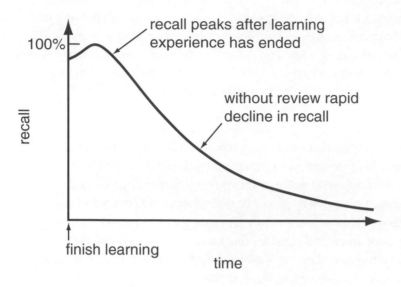

Without review, information is forgotten almost immediately.

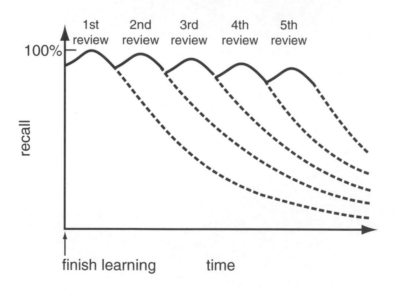

Recall is dramatically improved with regular review.

9   Recall is improved when information is regularly reviewed

Anyone who has ever taught must, at some time, have experienced the frustration of discovering that the entire class has apparently forgotten all of the material covered in the previous lesson. It is a feeling that is considerably accentuated if the previous lesson took place only the day before!

Yet, far from feeling surprised and frustrated by this, we should expect it, as we now know that *without review, information is forgotten almost immediately*.

This is illustrated by the upper graph opposite, which supports the finding that within 24 hours of a lesson ending, upwards of 80 per cent of the material covered is 'lost'. If this is what happens in the space of 24 hours it is little wonder that students often struggle to recall information up to a week later and have even greater difficulties in examinations that occur weeks and even months after the original learning event.

The good news is that *by regularly reviewing information, recall can be dramatically improved*. The lower graph opposite demonstrates the significant improvement in recall brought about by reviewing the material at regular intervals after the learning experience. It is not particularly time consuming – reviewing information takes around five minutes – nor is there any trick involved. It is simply an effective strategy for boosting recall and a habit well worth developing in students.

Implications for learning
You will notice from the graphs opposite that retention rates are greatest shortly *after* the learning experience has ended, which is as a result of the brain subconsciously processing information. This is the optimum time for the first review. Unfortunately, this peak occurs approximately ten minutes after an hour-long lesson has ended – just when students are starting their next lessons or are rushing for their lunch! To get around this problem, finish a few minutes early and spend the end of your lesson reviewing what has been learned.

It is only necessary for students to review the *key points*, which they themselves should identify, as opposed to the entire lesson. Spend around five minutes going over these points, preferably in a variety of different ways. For example, you could ask students to:

- translate the key written points into diagrammatic form
- verbalize the key points either to a neighbour or quietly to themselves
- pick out the keywords and write them in different colours
- turn the keywords into a mnemonic or acronym.

By combining words with images and colours, both hemispheres of the brain are engaged, ensuring that memory is enhanced (see page 45).

Trying to learn without reviewing is like trying to fill the bath without putting the plug in.

The review process must be repeated 24 hours later, and again after one week and after one month. A final review three months after the original learning experience will help cement the new knowledge and information into the long-term memory. At these subsequent reviews, encourage students to try to recall the key points – or write them on a piece of paper – before looking at their original notes. Again, changing the form in which the key points are recorded contributes to the process of committing information to the long-term memory.

Just as the enhanced opportunities afforded by the beginning of the lesson are often wasted (see page 37), so too are the opportunities to cement information by a process of review at the end of the lesson. Instead, the end of the lesson can all too easily become a time for collecting resources and hurriedly giving out homework as the thoughts of the students quickly turn to football practice or the lunch menu.

Not only is the end of the lesson the *prime* opportunity for review, which we would all do well to exploit, it is the opportunity over which the teacher retains the greatest degree of control. Subsequent reviews are far more heavily dependent upon the individual student. The beginning of the next lesson does, however, provide one further opportunity for the teacher to ensure that students review the key points. It can be effective to get students into the habit of starting every lesson by spending a few minutes reviewing the previous lesson's work – as the teacher prepares to begin the new learning experience with a dramatic and unusual delivery of *this* lesson's key learning point (see pages 37 and 49).

Students should be encouraged to review their work as a matter of course and, as with many habits, it is often easier to develop at an early age. Many students will be persuaded to regularly review their work if they see it is having a beneficial effect upon their learning and recall. They will also be encouraged that they are no longer being asked to spend hours reading pages of notes: review only takes five minutes!

Reviewing

1 The first review should take place at the end of the lesson.

2 Students identify the key point(s) of the lesson – around three is sufficient.

3 These are recorded in words and images – preferably a combination of both. Small 'postcards' are useful for this purpose.

4 Verbalizing the points, either to themselves or their neighbours, enhances memory.

5 Students should review their key points a day later – it only takes five minutes! Students should try to write the key points out, before they look at their notes. It is also helpful for the form of the key points to be changed: for example, students could convert a word into an image.

6 A following review should take place one week later, or at the start of the next lesson.

7 Further reviews should take place after one month and three months. They need only last for five minutes.

When students can't see the point of learning - when they don't want to learn - they almost certainly won't.

10   People learn best when they want to learn

When students can't see the point of learning – when they don't want to learn – they almost certainly won't. Motivation is therefore very important for effective learning. If we can create an environment in which students *want* to learn, then we have done the hard part: the learning will flow quite naturally.

I vividly recall teaching a Year 8 class and beginning the lesson by asking them what they wanted to know about the North Sea. 'Absolutely nothing', came back the honest answer, from a young girl sitting near the back. It is an example that illustrates the problem that all teachers face on a regular basis – how to encourage students to learn when they struggle to see any relevance in the material. The issue of relevance is one over which we, as teachers, have limited control.

Motivation is highly personal. People learn best when they know why they are learning and this will be different for every student in the class. It may well be that students are motivated to learn because they want to do well in their exams. Often we have to look beyond GCSE, however: a student may want exam success because it is the passport to becoming a pilot, for example, and *that* is what really motivates them. Encouraging students to identify *why* they are learning – sometimes referred to as the, 'what's in it for me' factor – is an important first step in the learning process.

Implications for learning

Students should be helped to identify their personal learning goals at the beginning of a learning experience. Too often goals are provided for students, the underlying assumption being that all of them are motivated by examination and academic success. The factors that motivate a particular student may well be very different to those that motivated and continue to motivate the teacher. Goals are important in the learning process, but are only effective if they have been set and are therefore valued by the individual. Encourage your students to begin each lesson by completing the phrase, 'By the end of this lesson, I will have ...'. A goal sends an important message to the brain: 'Let me in, I'm worth learning!'

Of course, we cannot make people *want* to learn, any more than we can make them learn. All teachers have encountered students who have successfully resisted all attempts at motivation and remain determined not to learn. Often, we are struggling against an unsupportive home background, where learning and achievement have been consistently undervalued and have led to years of failure in the classroom.

Motivating students, although undeniably difficult, is the key to learning. The fact that it is so very personal means that there is not one single fool-proof strategy that will ensure that all students are miraculously motivated – if only it were that easy! However, we significantly increase the chances of motivating students, when:

● *They feel that they have some control over their learning*. This can be established by providing students with some choice over both what they learn and how they learn it. For example, the teacher could invite students to 'choose either exercise A or exercise B' or to 'either draw a labelled diagram or write a short paragraph'. The feeling of having no control over their learning is a major source of negative stress in students, and therefore a significant barrier to learning in the classroom.

What motivates your students?

Have you ever asked them?

- *They feel that they are being challenged.* While too much challenge is likely to result in immediate demotivation, and insufficient challenge is almost certain to induce boredom, providing the appropriate level of challenge for all students will be highly motivating. Challenges, such as 'I bet you can't think of five reasons why...', can be provided to individuals, pairs or small groups.

- *They feel that they have some input into their learning.* Lessons can all too easily, and unintentionally, block out the learner, with information given and answers provided in such a way that the student has little opportunity to contribute. Students like to feel fully involved in the learning process and feel that their contribution is valued. If they are precluded from participating, they are likely to become demotivated and 'switch off'.

- *They feel that they are succeeding.* Success breeds success. Similarly, nothing de-motivates like failure, particularly if it is consistent and predictable. The fact that success is such a key to motivation demands that teachers seek to create opportunities for all students to be successful. Success is a reason to praise, and praise and attention, in whatever form, are things that we all respond to.

- *They feel that there is hope.* Hope means that they have a chance of learning, achieving and succeeding, and is an emotion that teachers must protect at all costs. For without hope, all is lost: motivation evaporates and learning is out of the question. Students must feel safe before they can learn. They must feel that they have 'permission to fail' but that, ultimately, the teacher both *wants* them to succeed and *believes* that they can do so! Ban the phrase, 'I can't', from your classroom and replace it with, 'I *can* do this, with a little help'.

If motivation is the key to learning, negative emotions are the biggest threat to students learning effectively. Students who are angry, depressed, upset or preoccupied, will not learn. They cannot: the emotion is simply a barrier that will not allow the learning brain to function. Frequently, it is not anything that the teacher does that causes these emotions. They are brought to the lesson, often from home. Although as teachers we have little or no control over the emotional state of our students on arrival, we must accept that, unless they are in the correct emotional state, they will not learn anything.

> **Our first task when students arrive at our classroom is to get them in an appropriate emotional state to learn.**

- **What have your students understood?**

- **How do you know?**

- **How much will they remember?**

PART TWO: WHAT MAKES A GOOD LESSON?

Lessons are for learning

> *Let me nail my colours to the mast: lessons are for learning...*
>
> *Children should leave a classroom at the end of a lesson knowing, understanding and being able to do more than when they came in. If we achieve that, then we are doing our job. Consequently, both as a reminder and an instantaneous, if somewhat simplistic, self-evaluation, 'WHAT HAVE THEY LEARNED?' is the question that should be on every teacher's lips at the end of every lesson.*
>
> *It is a crude analysis, but if I am guilty of stating the obvious and oversimplifying the issue, I offer no apology as I can think of no more appropriate gauge for how effective a lesson has been, if only as a rule of thumb. It is also precisely the simple, unambiguous benchmark that is required as a salutary reminder that lessons should be all about learning.*
>
> Extract from *Lessons are for Learning* by Mike Hughes
> (Network Educational Press, 1997)

'How is this activity helping students learn?' This is the question that I constantly ask as I teach or observe a lesson. The fact that I sometimes struggle to answer it is indicative of the Learning Gap that is often evident in the classroom.

For learning is not the same thing as being occupied, sitting quietly or producing copious notes. Learning involves *memory and understanding*. Students can leave the classroom with more notes than when they entered and with exercises successfully completed, but if they do not understand and do not remember, then they haven't learned – and learning is what lessons are, or at least should be, all about.

Understanding
Understanding is a precious commodity – the Holy Grail of the classroom, to be pursued, nurtured and cherished – because without it, there can be no genuine learning. Understanding is the moment at which the fog clears, everything 'clicks' and the brain silently exclaims 'ah ha!' It is the deeply personal moment at which the brain finally makes sense of something, which, from that point on, begins to become easy.

Beware the impostor, though, because much can masquerade as understanding. Pages of notes, particularly when they are written neatly, can be a convincing disguise. We *must* be vigilant, and ask at every opportunity, *'how is this helping them understand?'*

> **Understanding is not a luxury or additional bonus: it is our conscious goal.**
>
> **Neither is it something that happens by chance: it needs to be encouraged and developed.**

Learning is not done to people. It is done by them.

Making sense, personal sense, of something is the very essence of understanding. It is something that the brain does efficiently and naturally, the role of the teacher being to provide the initial stimulus and to point the brain in the right direction. Classroom activities need to be selected carefully with this in mind and tasks must be set that require the student to delve, explore, apply, sort, simplify and consider 'why' as well as 'what'.

Crucially, *we must challenge students to think*, for without thinking, consciously or otherwise, there is no sense and without the brain making sense, there is no understanding.

Above all, understanding is the product of *doing*, yet all too often students sit in the classroom and receive, with little being required of them other than listening, writing notes and completing low level comprehension exercises. They receive large amounts of information but are less frequently required to do any thing with it. Consequently, there is little need to think and the brain is not stimulated to make sense. Tasks may therefore be completed successfully, but fail to fully develop the understanding that is a pre-requisite of genuine learning.

Similarly, lessons that involve little *doing* give only limited opportunities for students to demonstrate, even to themselves, what they have understood. It is easy to gauge how much has been written; it is a completely different issue to assess how much has been understood. Lessons are for learning, yet it is all too easy for lessons to pass, both without very much learning taking place and without the teacher knowing what an individual student has learned.

Remembering

Not only is *doing* a catalyst for understanding, it also plays a key role in the memory, by providing the context that is required to activate the brain's natural memory systems. We should not underestimate the importance of making the learning experience memorable, for understanding and memory are not the same and there seems little point striving so hard to develop understanding if what has been understood cannot be retrieved.

For while understanding will significantly increase the chances of something being remembered, it does not guarantee it. Making our lessons memorable, by providing dramatic, unusual and unexpected experiences, heavily embedded in context, must be our second, separate, albeit related, goal.

An effective way of ensuring that information is remembered is by teaching it. Only around five per cent of what is heard and ten per cent of what is read is remembered, but around 90 per cent of what is taught is remembered. This figure can be explained by the fact that the contributory factors necessary in both understanding and memory are an integral part of the process of teaching.

Preparing to teach involves simplifying and making personal sense of the material – this helps understanding. Then the act of teaching provides a context and ensures that we are doing something with what we have learned soon after learning it – this is a memory aid. In effect we are reviewing our learning and making it stick.

Shut your eyes: picture your perfect lesson.

Make it as real as possible. Include as much detail as you can. Start from the time students enter the classroom and work your way through to the end of the lesson. Try to involve all five senses.

Now, consider the following questions:

- What did the room look like?

- What was on the walls?

- How was the furniture arranged?

- Where was the teacher's desk? Was there one?

- How were the students greeted – with a smile?

- How did the lesson start?

- How long did the introduction last?

- How many activities were included in the lesson?

- What were they?

- How did they engage the students? What were they required to do?

- How did the lesson end?

Describe your picture in detail to at least three people.

Repeat this exercise after you have finished reading this book.

My picture of a perfect lesson

As the students approach the classroom they are relaxed and happy: this is a lesson they obviously enjoy. The teacher is standing by the doorway. She is smiling and greets the class with a warm, 'Good morning' as they enter the room. The students smile back and respond to her questions and comments addressed to individual children: 'I see that the Under 14s had a good win last night Rachel, how many did you score?'; 'I enjoyed listening to the Swing Band in assembly this morning Jonathon, how long had you been practising that piece for?'

The first thing that I notice as I look around is how bright and cheerful the room is. There are posters and displays of work done by students all around the room, with many of the keywords and phrases associated with the subject written in large and colourful letters. The display on the front wall, which the class looks at more than any other, is particularly attractive.

The students that arrived early have already settled and are reviewing the three 'key points' that they had identified from the previous lesson. When everyone has entered the room, the teacher beckons to a student to collect a large notice from the front of the classroom and hang it on the outside of the door: it reads, 'Do not disturb – learning in progress.'

No more than three minutes have passed when the teacher asks each student to decide which of their three key points from the last lesson is the most important, and to tell the person sitting next to them. As the students exchange this information, their partners respond with the question, 'Why?' It is apparent that the group has done this exercise on previous occasions.

Just as the class completes this exercise, the teacher jumps onto a desk near the front of the room and begins to peel an orange, letting the pieces fall into a huge box marked 'jigsaw' that is on the floor. The entire class is intrigued and watches the teacher's performance spellbound.

With the orange almost peeled, the teacher outlines in very general terms what the lesson is going to be about, before explaining in a little more detail what each student should have achieved by the end of the lesson. If, for the purpose of this picture, the exact content of the lesson is not significant, the phrases used by the teacher most certainly are: 'By the end of this lesson you will all know the following three things...'; 'Make sure that you know the difference between ... before you leave the room.' One student writes these phrases down on a large piece of paper, quietly leaves his seat and attaches it to the door.

(continue on page 67)

Checklist of components of effective learning:

■ welcome from the teacher

■ stimulating environment

■ relaxed but challenging atmosphere

■ effective beginning

■ unusual, unexpected activity

■ more than one activity

■ variety of activities

■ students are engaged – required to do

■ reflection/review built in.

*As the lesson progresses, the students are engaged in a variety of activities, none lasting longer than 15 minutes and each very different to the previous one. Students are required to write, to listen, to visualize and to draw. Frequently they talk to their partners and occasionally break into small groups to discuss the matter in hand. Above all they are required to **do**, to engage and to think.*

As I watch, I notice that individual students appear to enjoy some activities more than others, but the sheer variety of the tasks ensures that there is something for everyone. I particularly notice a boy sitting near the back, who has appeared a little restless for much of the lesson, and the enthusiasm with which he approaches the task of turning the diagram in the book into a 30-second play.

A student seeks the attention of the teacher saying, 'I know I can do this but I'm going to need some extra help', and I am struck by the fact that no one has used the phrase, 'I can't'. This does not mean that no one is seeking assistance and clarification: on the contrary, there is an almost constant dialogue between the teacher and members of the group. Rather it indicates that the expectations of both teacher and students are high.

There is evidence of pace, involvement and above all enjoyment, as students are challenged without being placed under undue and unnecessary pressure. Approximately halfway through the lesson, the teacher calls, 'Time-out'. The student's response indicates that this is something they are used to. Some sit and talk to a friend, others get up and 'stretch their legs', while a few talk to the teacher about a forthcoming trip. All – teacher and students – appear very much refreshed when they resume their work.

As the lesson nears the end, the teacher asks the class to clear away the materials they have been using. This they do with the minimum of fuss and then sit waiting for their next instruction, realizing that the lesson was not yet over. The teacher invites the students to shut their eyes if they wish while they reflect in silence on the lesson that has just passed. They are then asked to identify the three most important things they have learned during the lesson. Some write them down on a postcard, some draw a simple diagram, while some do neither – then they all share their thoughts with the person sitting next to them. There is considerable agreement over the first two points although there is some vigorous discussion over the third point.

Meanwhile, the teacher has removed the piece of paper from the door, which outlines the three things that everyone should know before they leave the room. She draws the student's attention to the sheet and invites everyone to check that they have achieved the objectives. A couple of correctly answered questions and a quiet word with one or two students seem to satisfy the teacher that the lesson has been a success.

The bell goes and the teacher thanks the class for their contributions and tells them how much she has enjoyed working with them. She gives a final reminder that the students should review their key learning points when they get home and again tomorrow, and the class begins to drift out. They return the teacher's smile and thank her for the lesson before saying their goodbyes.

Establishing the goal is an often neglected but all-important first step to improvement.

Without it, we can neither set our course nor measure our progress.

Aiming to improve

It is not sufficient to exhort teachers to get better. Even when people accept the need to improve, and have the desire to do so, they have to be clear about precisely what they are trying to achieve before they can. In order to get better we have to be able to see the destination. Otherwise we can neither set our course, nor measure our progress.

In recent years, the lack of such a goal has hindered the national development of teaching quality – a situation that has been compounded by the mixed messages that teachers have had to interpret. Teachers could be forgiven for looking towards OFSTED – whose business it is to judge the quality of teaching – for the goal. They would be disappointed, however, as the criteria by which OFSTED judges teaching are vague, short on the 'how' and skirt around the key purpose of teaching, which is learning.

It's not that teachers would necessarily disagree with any of the OFSTED criteria for evaluating teaching, but rather that they fall somewhat short of providing the goal for which teachers should aim. We teach in order to help our students learn and yet the word 'learning' fails to appear in the OFSTED criteria.

Not only have teachers lacked a goal in recent years, they have been confused by a series of mixed messages received from government policies, politicians in general and the media. Teachers have been asked to wade through an overcrowded curriculum and are being held increasingly accountable for the proportion of students who perform well, in absolute terms, in public examinations. They have also heard and read scathing attacks on 'trendy teaching methods' (whatever they are) and heard long and loud calls for a return to the 'basics'.

However, they are also conscious that the students they are currently teaching will spend their adult lives living and working in the twenty first century. They are aware that their lives will be characterized by instant global communications, rapid access to unlimited information and frequent job changes. We stand at the threshold of the 'Information Society', and the 'Learning Age' that it will spawn. Today's children will be doing the jobs not yet invented; they will need to be flexible, autonomous and ready and able to continue learning throughout their lives.

There are many people who find these two messages contradictory and confusing: are teachers being asked to transfer the contents of a syllabus and prepare students to pass exams or are they being asked to help prepare young people for the very different demands of the next century?

Little wonder, then, that teachers are confused, and need clarification of exactly what they are trying to do in the classroom before they can make significant progress. It is precisely this ambiguity that makes the significant, but often neglected, step of 'establishing the goal' even more important.

The goal:

- **gives teachers something to aim for**

- **should focus on learning**

- **provides a checklist for observation**

- **provides a checklist for feedback**

- **can be subject and context specific**

- **is of more use when generated by a team of teachers.**

The goal

The goal should be a clear, concise statement outlining precisely what it is you are trying to achieve in the classroom.

The goal:

- *Gives teachers something to aim for.* It is difficult to improve without a specific goal. Many teachers find it useful to stick the goal to their desk as a constant reminder of what they are trying to achieve in the classroom.

- *Should focus upon effective learning.* Too many 'teaching and learning policies' concentrate upon teaching at the expense of learning. Typically, policies reflect the OFSTED criteria, emphasizing the importance of the teacher arriving for the lesson on time, having clear objectives and being well prepared. They also outline in some detail the resources that students are required to bring to the lesson and how they are expected to set out their work. While these are important features of effective lessons, they are insufficient, as they do not focus directly upon the learning process. Ironically, it may be possible for a lesson to comply with all the criteria set out in a teaching and learning policy, and for very little, if any, learning to actually take place! Lessons are for learning and this should be reflected by the goal.

- *Provides a checklist for observation.* It is a central argument of this book that observation alone is relatively ineffective. A goal can help provide a focus for observation. In short, it helps the observer to know exactly what he or she is looking for.

- *Provides a checklist for feedback.* Feedback too can be focused upon previously agreed criteria.

- *Can be subject specific.* The wide range and very different natures of secondary school subjects can be taken into account if 'learning goals' are established in subject teams.

- *Is of more use when generated by a team of teachers,* as opposed to being imposed 'from above'. Not only is the process beneficial – it will generate thought and discussion about the whole issue of classroom practice – people are more likely to be receptive to feedback about their performance when it is related to criteria that they themselves have agreed to.

- *Can improve consistency within a department.* If all teachers have had the opportunity to discuss the issue and contribute towards the goal, there is a greater chance of reaching an agreement across the department about what is effective practice. Even in circumstances where it is not possible to reach total agreement, participation in the process increases the collective understanding of what colleagues in the department consider to be effective. The chances then of students having a similar experience in a particular subject, irrespective of their teacher, are enhanced.

Establishing your goal

■ **Effective learning takes place when:**

```

```

■ **Children learn effectively in (science) when:**

```

```

■ **The key features of an effective (science) lesson are:**

```

```

■ **The differences between a good (science) lesson and an excellent one are:**

```

```

It is important to be bold when establishing your goal. Be careful not to confuse what you currently do with what you would like to do or what you could do.

Establishing your goal

By focusing our attention upon *learning* when setting out the goal, we are able to reach beneath the sterile and superficial debate about whether whole-class teaching to children sitting silently in rows is more effective than allowing children to sit and work together in small groups.

By focusing upon *teaching* and *styles* at the expense of *learning*, the so-called 'Teaching and Learning Styles debate', which has raged unabated for over two decades, has been misleading, distracting and particularly unhelpful. It has also consistently missed the point. Teaching is *not* an end in itself. We teach in order to help students learn and it is learning that should therefore be the centre of our attention when establishing the goal.

There is no single correct, most effective way of teaching. Good teachers need a repertoire of styles and an extensive range of strategies. They also need a comprehensive understanding about how their students learn and a clear picture of the environment and conditions they must establish in their classrooms in order to facilitate effective learning.

Similarly, *there is no single correct way of establishing the goal*. The important thing is that a goal is established and that teachers are fully involved in the process. The approaches described in this book are no more than suggestions and should be adapted to fit particular circumstances and specific needs.

1   An effective way of generating discussion and debate, and ultimately of establishing your goal, is to use prompts that teachers are asked to complete. An exercise such as this can be used as part of an INSET session or departmental meeting and can be completed individually or in small groups.

2   Ask teachers to consider and respond to *one* of the prompts opposite. The agreed response of the department as a whole forms a statement that can be used as the basis for a learning policy and provides the goal towards which teachers can aim. In order to keep the statement manageable and concise, limit the response to around six bullet points.

3   If you, as an individual or as a group, are having difficulty completing this task, try inverting the prompt statement. For example, consider the conditions that are *not conducive* to learning and the practices that lead to *ineffective* learning. Often, this strategy can give the necessary impetus to a group discussion that is in danger of stagnating.

4   Having completed the statement and established your goal, the next challenge is to recreate the environment and experiences that you agree help children learn effectively, in every lesson!

Children learn effectively when they:

- **want to**

- **are relaxed, yet alert**

- **are learning in their preferred style**

- **are actively engaged i.e. doing something**

- **encounter something unusual, dramatic and unexpected**

- **regularly review what they have learned.**

Children learn effectively when they...	So we must...
want to	<ul><li>encourage them to set personal goals</li><li>help them see the benefits of learning</li><li>provide some element of choice</li></ul>
are relaxed, yet alert	<ul><li>smile!</li><li>greet students as they enter the classroom</li><li>provide a stimulating learning environment</li><li>avoid putting children 'on the spot'</li><li>endeavour to create challenge rather than stress</li><li>provide some element of choice</li></ul>
are learning in their preferred styles	<ul><li>include a variety of learning activities in every lesson</li><li>include visual, auditory and kinesthetic activities – preferably in every lesson, but at the very least in every unit of work</li><li>be aware that not every student will be learning effectively during any given activity</li></ul>

(continued on the next page)

Children learn effectively when they...	So we must...
are actively engaged i.e. *doing* something	<ul><li>provide activities that require students to 'make sense of something'</li><li>encourage children to develop understanding</li><li>encourage children to demonstrate their understanding</li><li>encourage students to 'use their understanding'</li></ul>
encounter something unusual, dramatic and unexpected	<ul><li>exploit the opportunity at the beginning of the lessons to capture students' interest</li><li>identify the key learning point of each lesson and find different ways of covering it</li><li>identify the key learning point in each unit of work and make a conscious effort to introduce it in an unusual way</li></ul>
regularly review what they have learned	<ul><li>make good use of the last ten minutes of a lesson</li><li>encourage students to identify the key point(s) in each lesson</li><li>encourage students to systematically review their key points one day, one week and one month after the lesson</li><li>start each lesson by reviewing the last</li></ul>

From 'what' to 'how' to 'when'

While establishing the goal is a crucial first step, to decide *what* we are trying to do in the classroom, it in no way guarantees that it will be achieved. It has to be quickly followed by consideration of precisely *how* we are going to create the desirable conditions in the classroom. This is most effectively done when teams of teachers work collaboratively to draw upon their collective expertise and creativity.

Then, having established *how* we might ensure that students are learning effectively, consideration must be given to *when* we can include various strategies in our teaching programme, by identifying suitable opportunities in our schemes of work.

It is the failure to follow this process through the second and third steps that is a major reason why so many of the developments in our understanding of the learning process fail to find their way into the classroom. Teachers are often aware of *what* it is they could do to make learning more effective but are unsure *how* this translates into lesson activities.

The key is to be as precise and specific as possible and to ensure that the agreed features of effective learning and appropriate lesson activities are written into schemes of work.

This point is best illustrated by working through an actual example.

What
We identify the 'what' when we establish the goal. This is best done when teams of teachers respond to one of the prompts suggested on page 72.

In *Lessons are for Learning* (Network Educational Press, 1997), the prompt 'Children learn effectively when they...' produced the following response:

Children learn effectively when they:

- are interested in and enjoy what they are doing – when lessons are memorable
- ask, as opposed to answer, questions
- are challenged to think about the work they are doing
- understand what they are learning
- receive individual help and attention.

I do not claim that this is the 'correct answer' to this prompt: it is simply *my* goal. The next challenge is to create these conditions in the classroom, and so attention must turn to 'how'.

From 'what' to 'how' to 'when'

Establish the goal

What are we trying to achieve?

↓

Translate this into lesson activities

How are we going to do it?

↓

Look for opportunities to use them

When are we going to do it?

How

Take each of the component parts of your goal in turn and consider in some detail how it could be achieved in the classroom.

Think about what kinds of activities could best deliver each objective. Again, this is best done collaboratively by using prompts such as the one below.

Children are challenged to think about material when they are required to:

- apply it
- reduce it
- change it
- teach it
- simplify it
- summarize it.

This list is not exhaustive; simply the outcome of a recent INSET session that I attended.

The requirements identified now need to be translated into learning activities. Ideas for two points from the list above are given below.

'Reduce it'
- Reduce a paragraph to six words by identifying the six words that *you* consider to be the most important.
- Reduce three sides of notes to 50 words.
- '*Romeo and Juliet*' has to be reduced by four minutes for television purposes. Achieve this by eliminating part or all of a scene. You must, however, make sure that you do not lose any of the meaning of the play.

'Change it'
- Describe a picture in words.
- Turn a piece of text into a diagram.
- Paint a piece of music.
- Write about a graph.
- Make a model of something described in a piece of text.
- Turn a piece of text into a 30-second play.

Writing effective learning activities into schemes of work increases the chances of the 'what' described in your goal actually finding its way into the classroom.

When

Once you have decided upon suitable and effective learning activities, look for occasions when you can use them. When you have identified such opportunities, write the activities into your schemes of work. By including them as suggested activities in this way, you increase the likelihood of teachers actually employing them during lessons, and therefore increase the chances of the 'what' you have so carefully identified in your goal actually finding its way into the classroom.

For example, a geography teacher might decide, having identified the paragraph below as being suitable for such an activity, that students could reduce a passage to six key words during a lesson covering exfoliation (during the Year 8 unit on Natural Processes).

> *'Onion skin weathering or exfoliation is a type of weathering commonly found in deserts. During the day the Sun heats up the rock causing it to expand, but at night it becomes cold and the rock contracts. Continual expansion and contraction gradually weakens the rock until eventually bits break or peel off, like the skin of an onion.'*
>
> **Task**: *Reduce this paragraph to six words by selecting the six words that you consider to be the most important.*

This task can be done individually, in small groups or as a whole-class activity. The task of selecting just six words requires discussion, but above all, considerable thought – a typical Year 8 group would throw up 10–14 words. Students should be able to justify their chosen words and explain why they have not considered other words important enough to include in their list.

Using this exercise, the teacher is doing more than teaching about exfoliation: he is teaching the basics of note-taking. Most importantly, he is challenging students to think and thereby deepen their understanding.

Many learning activities, including those mentioned here, could of course be used effectively on many occasions. Writing suggested tasks and activities into schemes of work is not intended to restrict teachers or reduce their flexibility; only to encourage all teachers to employ a range of agreed strategies, when otherwise they might not.

It is useful for teachers to be equipped with a range of generic strategies, which they can apply as and when they consider them appropriate. By identifying strategies, rather than simply concentrating upon content, teachers can pick up good ideas from each other and will particularly benefit from working from colleagues who teach in a different style to themselves. Keep a range of 'good ideas for lessons' in the front of your planner or stuck to your desk, and select the activity most suitable for the content and learning objective of each particular lesson.

In order to establish precisely what is happening in your classroom, ask yourself:

■ **What do I do in the classroom?**

■ **How effectively does what I do help students to learn?**

Section Two

The state of play

The aim of this section is to help you reflect upon what is happening in your classroom, in order to establish your Learning Gap.

WHAT IS GOING ON IN YOUR CLASSROOM?

The pace at which teachers are forced to conduct their professional lives is not conducive to regular reflection upon what it is they actually do and how effective their current practice is. This, however, is a crucial step in establishing the Learning Gap.

'What is going on in your classroom?' is a question that you cannot answer accurately alone. For example, a teacher's perception of what is happening during a lesson is often totally different from what the students think is happening. A systematic approach is therefore required, involving data and objective feedback, in order to complement the process of self-reflection and establish an accurate picture of the way in which we teach.

There are two distinct questions that teachers need to address in order to evaluate the effectiveness of their current practice and to establish their personal Learning Gap.

1   *What do I do in the classroom?* Which teaching strategies and learning activities do I frequently employ? How long do I talk for? What is the normal pattern of my lessons?

2   *How effectively does what I do help students to learn?*

If the purpose of a lesson is to help students learn, we must carefully examine our current practice and evaluate the extent to which the strategies that we employ during lessons are conducive to learning. The 'scatter-graph activity' that first appeared in the author's *'Lessons are for Learning'* (Network Educational Press, 1997) is outlined in the following pages (84 and 85). It is intended to help teachers reflect upon what they currently do in the classroom and the effectiveness of their practice. Although it can be completed individually, it can be more effective to work collaboratively on this activity in subject teams, drawing upon information generated from observation to establish what happens in the classroom, and discussing the relative merits of various teaching strategies. Of particular interest will be the trend line on your graph and any pattern revealed by the data. Are the strategies that you frequently use in your classroom the ones that you believe are the most effective in helping children to learn? If not, why not?

It may be of interest to compare your completed scatter graph with the graph on page 87. This graph represents the combined responses of over 500 students, aged 11–16, taken from a wide variety of secondary schools. While it may lack something in terms of academic research, it provides an interesting snapshot of what young people believe is happening during lessons, and it should not be dismissed lightly. If nothing else, it provides a 'student's eye view' that should encourage teachers to reflect upon their own classrooms as they seek to establish their Learning Gap.

Lesson activity frequency checklist

Step 1	Below is a list of commonly employed teaching strategies. Award each a mark out of ten depending on how frequently you use the particular strategy in your teaching. (10 = frequently. 1 = very rarely.) Try to use the full range of marks.
Step 2	Give each strategy a second mark out of ten, depending on how effectively you think it contributes to learning. (10 = significant contribution to learning. 1 = minimal contribution to learning.)
Step 3	Plot your results on the scatter graph axes opposite.
Step 4	Consider your completed scatter graph. Are the strategies that you consider the most effective in helping children learn the ones that you employ the most frequently?

Lesson activity	Frequency (1-10)	Learning (1-10)
Reading		
Answering questions from a book		
Individual help and guidance		
Copying from the board		
Observing demonstrations		
Dictation		
Practical work		
Answering questions from the board		
Writing notes		
Listening to the teacher		
Answering the teacher's questions		
Class discussion		
Watching videos		
Groupwork		
Individual projects/research		
Working in pairs		
Reporting to the rest of the group		
Talking to other pupils		
Educational visits		
Guest speakers		
Simulations/role play		
'Fill in the blanks' exercises		

Lesson Activities : Relationship between frequency of use and perceived effectiveness in developing learning

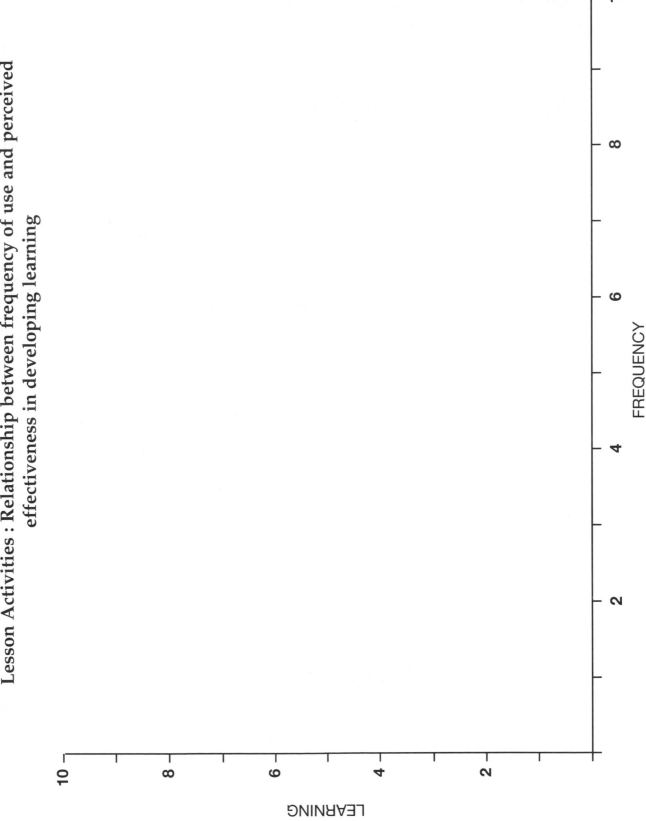

FREQUENCY

LEARNING

Reflect on your personal scatter graph:

- Can you identify any trend?

- Do you frequently employ the strategies that you believe are effective in helping students learn? If not, why not?

- Do you employ strategies that you believe are relatively ineffective in promoting learning?

- How frequently do you employ these strategies?

- Why do you employ them at all?

Lesson Activities : Relationship between frequency of use and perceived effectiveness in developing learning

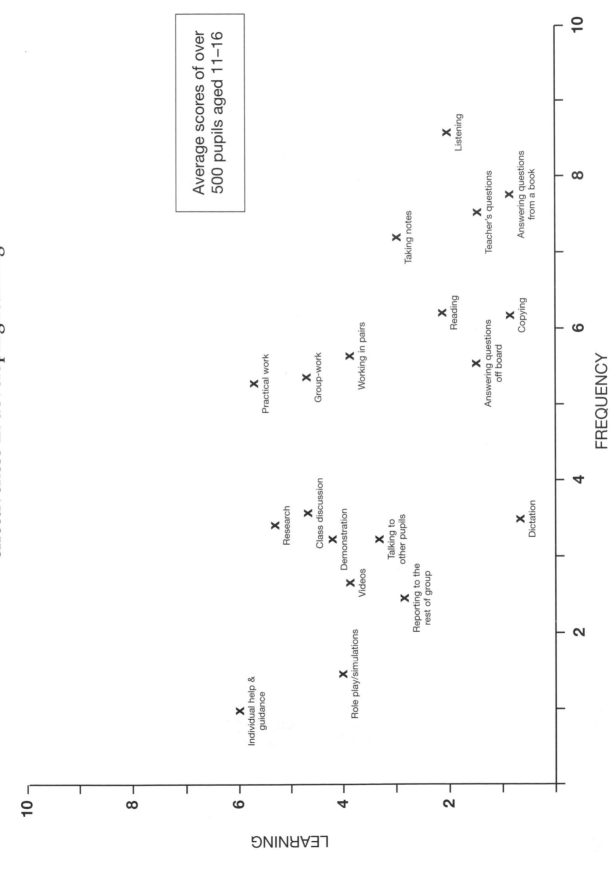

Average scores of over 500 pupils aged 11–16

LEARNING

FREQUENCY

Individual help & guidance

Role play/simulations

Research

Class discussion

Demonstration

Videos

Talking to other pupils

Reporting to the rest of group

Practical work

Group-work

Working in pairs

Dictation

Reading

Answering questions off board

Copying

Taking notes

Teacher's questions

Answering questions from a book

Listening

What have they learned?

This is the question that should be on every teacher's lips at the end of every lesson.

The next part of this section is structured around ten characteristic features of current classroom practice, which are listed below. It is designed to encourage further thought and reflection about the extent to which the way we teach helps our students learn.

It is a personal view based upon first hand experiences in countless classrooms in a wide variety of secondary schools, and is inevitably, therefore, confined to generalizations. Some of them you may recognize, while some of them will be unfamiliar to you. To a certain extent, what I have observed in other people's classrooms is relatively unimportant: it is what is going on in your lessons that is of significance to you, as you seek to establish your personal Learning Gap.

The current situation in many classrooms

1 Students spend the majority of their time reading, writing and listening.

2 Students answer a lot of questions.

3 The beginnings and ends of lessons are often wasted.

4 Activities – especially the introduction by the teacher – often last longer than the students' concentration spans.

5 Many lessons consist of a single main activity.

6 The 'key learning point' is often delivered in the middle of the lesson.

7 Lessons are highly predictable.

8 Students are often placed under negative stress.

9 Most lessons are forgotten within 24 hours.

10 Students are often bored.

- How much time do children spend reading, writing and listening in your lessons?

- How do you cater for the kinesthetic learners in your class? Do you know who they are?

- What is the balance between content and context memory in your lessons?

- Think of the last three lessons you taught. How did the activities help develop understanding? How did you assess what had been understood?

1 Children spend a lot of time reading, listening and writing

The scatter graph on page 87 appears to confirm both my own observations and my memories of secondary school: children spend large amounts of time in school reading, listening and writing.

Teachers often respond to this observation by pointing out that reading, listening and writing are efficient and effective ways of ensuring that the contents of a still-overcrowded National Curriculum or examination syllabus are covered and transferred from the teacher to the student. The fact that teachers are being placed under ever-increasing pressure, under the spotlight of public accountability, further encourages them to ensure not only that they have covered the syllabus but that they are able to prove it.

Yet the National Curriculum is not there simply to be covered: it is there to be *learned*. While reading, listening and writing may indeed enable teachers to transfer vast quantities of information relatively quickly, the extent to which they are employed as classroom strategies has some significant implications for learning.

Implications for learning
- *Kinesthetic learners are significantly disadvantaged* when they are required to spend the majority of their time reading, listening and writing. (These are students who prefer to learn by *doing* – touching, feeling, making. See page 41.)

  In a typical class, around one-third of the students will prefer to learn kinesthetically and although many of them will be able to adapt and learn outside of their preferred style, there will always be some who will not. Not only will these students be disadvantaged and their learning retarded, there is a significant danger that they will become restless and eventually disruptive.

- *Reading, listening and writing are activities that depend heavily upon content memory.* Not only does learning in this way rely to a great extent upon the motivation of the individual student, for the brain it is unnatural and therefore strictly limited. It is no surprise, therefore, that information learned in this way is not easily remembered.

  The lack of active participation in the learning process (*doing*) that often results when children spend an excessive time reading, listening and writing will almost certainly limit the amount of *context memory* that is activated by a particular lesson. In contrast to *content* memory, *context* memory is natural, has unlimited capacity and is the way in which the brain remembers best (see page 49).

- *Reading, listening and writing are predominately left-brain activities.* Teachers who overuse these strategies in the classroom risk failing to engage the whole brain in the learning process and so miss an opportunity to optimize learning (see page 45). The fact that the left hemisphere of the female generally operates at a quicker rate than that of the male means that boys are further disadvantaged during lessons that are dominated by listening and textbook activities.

The earthquake was caused by movement along the subduction zone. Here, the Cocos Oceanic plate meets the Pacific plate...

Q. What caused the earthquake?

A. The earthquake was caused by movement along the subduction zone.

(But what is a subduction zone?)

Reading, listening and writing are, of course, valid learning activities. However, it is when they are used as isolated tasks, as they often are, that teachers are limiting the involvement of the right brain. The use of text in combination with colour, visual images and rhythm ensures that the whole brain is engaged by the learning activity and learning is maximized.

● *It is often possible to successfully complete reading, listening and writing tasks, without fully understanding the material.*

Notes, taken from a textbook, the blackboard or given by the teacher, can be completed with relative ease but with no guarantee of understanding. However, this type of lesson is common, particularly at Key Stage 4 when teachers are often predominately concerned with syllabus coverage. The notes, which are often accompanied by an oral explanation, are expected to be learned at a later date, possibly for homework, or used as revision material.

Lessons such as these, which rely heavily upon content memory, primarily engage the left brain and severely disadvantage kinesthetic learners, are extremely unlikely to develop *understanding* in all or even most of the students. Furthermore, it is extremely difficult, arguably impossible, for the teacher to assess to what extent the material has been understood due to the restrictive nature of the task.

Understanding, it would seem, is not the principle motive behind these lessons: have you ever heard a teacher say, 'Don't worry if you don't understand it, just write it down so that you can revise from it later'?

● *Successfully completing classroom tasks without fully understanding the material* is not confined to note-taking exercises. Comprehension activities based upon textbooks, worksheets or the blackboard, are also frequently used as lesson activities, but again, there is no guarantee that they develop understanding, or allow students to demonstrate what understanding they have.

Try the exercise opposite: the text is taken from a geography textbook frequently used with students at both Key Stage 3 and Key Stage 4. Answering the question and completing the task is straightforward. Like so many lesson activities, all you have to do is search the text and use your common sense. Don't worry if you don't understand what a *subduction zone* is – because of the way the activity is structured, the teacher will never know!

The vast majority of questions asked in the classroom are 'closed' questions.

These essentially assess what the student has already learned, and contribute little to the continuing learning process.

2   Children answer a lot of questions

During the course of a typical week in secondary school, children answer a lot of questions. From the teacher, from the board, on a worksheet or in a textbook, the questions just keep on coming: and students are required to answer.

Not only are students faced with a large number of questions, they often encounter them at the beginning of a lesson, to both recap on previously covered material and to introduce the new topic.

There are clearly a number of reasons why a teacher might wish to ask questions during a lesson. For example, the teacher might want to:

- find out what students know
- find out what they have remembered
- review a previous lesson
- boost self-esteem (by directing a question at a student who you know will get it correct, in order to give you a chance of praising them for their success)
- challenge students to think and deepen their understanding.

All of these motives – and the list is not exhaustive – are legitimate uses of questioning. The key for the teacher is to be clear about precisely why he or she is asking a question; is it to assess what has already been learned, or to try to help the student to learn new information?

In 'Lessons are for Learning' (Network Educational Press, 1997), I suggested that a very high proportion of questions asked during lessons are primarily designed to assess what has *already* been learned and remembered. As such, the vast majority of questions used in secondary classrooms do little to help students learn *new* information. For example, when students correctly answer that:

- the Battle of Waterloo was is in 1815
- Lima is the capital of Peru
- angles of less than 90° are called acute angles

they clearly have already learned this information and are not learning anything new.

Of course, it is essential that teachers are aware of what students already know and how much they have remembered from previous lessons, and asking questions is a quick and efficient way of eliciting this information – I do not suggest otherwise. However, I do wish to raise two key concerns regarding the questioning that I regularly witness in secondary classrooms:

1   *Relatively few open questions are asked*. These are questions such as, 'What do you think might happen if… ', which challenge students to think, deepen their understanding and help them learn. The vast majority of questions that I hear during lessons – I would estimate well in excess of 90 per cent – are closed questions, and do little other than help the teacher assess what has already been learned.

Reflect upon your own lessons:

■ Why do you ask questions?

■ How do the questions you ask help students learn?

Be observed while you are teaching:

■ Every time you answer a question, the observer should write down O (open) or C (closed).

■ Alternatively, the observer could give each question a score of 0–5 depending upon how it contributes to learning.

Analyse the results:

■ What percentage of the questions that you asked were open (scored 3–5)?

■ What percentage of your questions were closed (scored 0–2)?

■ When do you tend to ask the open questions – at the start of the lesson or in the middle?

2   *Teachers are often unsure why they are asking questions.* It is easy to confuse questions that assess what people already know with the thought-provoking questions that help people learn. Teachers often tell me that they asked questions during a lesson in order to develop learning and understanding, when, in fact, the restrictive nature of the questions meant that students were drawing upon existing knowledge and still answering them correctly.

Implications for learning

- The high proportion of closed questions that are asked during lessons may well mean that students are learning a lot less than the teacher thinks. Closed questions that require the student to draw upon existing knowledge for the correct answer are essentially assessment tools.

- The beginnings of many lessons are characterized by a series of short, closed questions, designed to recap on the previous lesson. In many instances, no more than six students answer a question – often it is the same six every lesson. The first open question often arrives well into the lesson – around 25 minutes after the start. Not only is the optimum learning time at the beginning of the lesson 'wasted', the deep, thought-provoking questions arrive during the middle of the lesson. This is the worst possible time, coinciding with the period when the capacity to remember and learn is at its lowest and when even the most conscientious students are beginning to lose concentration (see page 37).

- When only a handful of students are volunteering answers to questions, teachers will often direct questions at particular students in order to 'encourage' them to participate in the lesson. When this is done, as it often is, at the beginning of the lesson, there is a real danger that the student will be placed under undue negative stress and will retreat into survival mode (see page 31). Students learn best in a state of 'relaxed alertness', which is not always induced by directing questions to them – some of which they may struggle to answer – at the very start of the lesson.

- Many of the questions that students are asked can be answered by searching the text for the necessary clue. These 'low level comprehension' exercises are common in many secondary textbooks and occupy a sizeable proportion of the student's week. As with the question about the cause of the earthquake used on pages 92 and 93, they can be successfully answered with no, or minimal, understanding. Not only do exercises such as these, even when completed 'correctly', give little insight into how much of the text the student has *understood*, they fail to make a substantial contribution to the ongoing *learning* process.

Make the most of the beginnings of your lessons:

- Start learning within five minutes of the bell going.

- Start learning within one minute of the class arriving.

- Identify the 'key learning point' of the lesson and start with it.

- Collect in homework in the middle of the lesson – use it as a break between the learning activities.

- Distribute resources before the class arrives.

- Train students to come in and prepare themselves for learning with a minimum of fuss.

- Train students to come in and immediately review their three key points from the previous lesson.

Closing the Learning Gap

3   The beginnings and ends of lessons are often wasted

The beginning and end of a lesson present golden opportunities both to learn and to consolidate what has been learned. They are opportunities that can easily be wasted.

Reflect on your own lessons. To what extent do you recognize the picture described below?

The students drift in and begin to settle, late comers are chastised and instructions are issued to take out exercise books and to sit quietly. Gradually a hush descends and the teacher reads out the register. Having done so, we can proceed to the business of the day, which invariably starts with collecting in last week's homework.

The 'handing-in-of-homework' is a ritual enacted in countless classrooms and, I suspect, has changed little over the years. The majority of students duly hand their homework assignments to the teacher while a handful, their identity coming as no great surprise, nervously explain why they have failed to complete the task. All have, at least in their opinions, a very good reason why they have been unable to do their homework, reasons that anyone who has taught for even a matter of weeks is thoroughly familiar with. The teacher – occasionally with amusement, often with annoyance and always with frustration – debates the validity of the reason with each individual for a moment or two, before issuing an appropriate sanction and a general reminder about the importance of homework. The ritual complete, the lesson can proceed.

We are now around eight minutes into the lesson, perhaps longer, and nothing has been learned. Worse still, students are already beginning to get restless; the sense of anticipation they felt as they entered the classroom, however slight, is fading fast. By the time the textbooks and other resources for the lesson have been given out – or, even worse, fetched from a neighbouring classroom – over ten minutes of the lesson have elapsed.

As the lesson draws to a close, students are dashing around, collecting in resources and packing away their belongings. Although attention is beginning to drift, homework is set; hurriedly, for the bell is now imminent. The bell rings and the class is reminded that this event is for the benefit of the teacher, not the students. They are dismissed with their thoughts already turning to football practice, meeting the boyfriend or getting to the front of the lunch queue. Not only are they unsure about their homework task, they are forgetting the lesson even before they have left the room!

Implications for learning
- The ten minutes at the start of the lesson, when the potential for learning is greatest have been wasted. People remember more from the beginning of a learning experience – the *primacy* effect (see page 37) – which makes the opening few minutes of a lesson the optimum learning time. Using this time to collect homework and distribute resources is a waste of this opportunity.

Make the most of the ends of your lessons:

- End early – don't try to cover too much.

- Spend some time in group or individual reflections.

- Ask each student to identify the three most important things they have learned – their key points.

- Ask each student to share their key points with their neighbours.

- Briefly discuss some of the key points as a class. Tell the students the three things you considered most important.

- Give students time to write down their three key points.

- The key points should be reduced as much as possible – preferably to keywords. Use colour and visual images.

- Encourage students to review their keywords for homework. They should review them again at the end of the day, 24 hours later, and one week later.

- All students have a sense of anticipation at the start of a lesson, with many asking, 'What are we doing today Miss?' immediately they enter the room. By the time the learning begins in the lesson described, this feeling is significantly reduced.

- Learning often begins in classrooms a full ten minutes after the lesson has started. This is the equivalent of almost one lesson per day, one school day per week and around 195 lessons per year spent doing nothing!

- A frantic rush at the end of the lesson means that the optimum time for reviewing and consolidating what has been learned is often lost. Without review – and the end of the lesson is the best time to start the review process – around 80 per cent of what has been covered will be lost within 24 hours (see page 53). It's like trying to fill the bath without putting the plug in!

Many teachers, of course, draw their lessons to a close by summarizing and reviewing what has been covered during the lesson. Similarly, many teachers are proficient in ensuring that their lessons start promptly and crisply. I am not suggesting otherwise, but simply encouraging teachers to reflect upon the extent to which they exploit the valuable opportunities presented by the beginnings and ends of lessons.

Consider the way in which you start *your* lessons:
1   How do you start your lessons, typically?
2   How would your students answer question 1?
3   What are the first three things that you do or say? Why?
4   How soon does learning start in your lesson – within five minutes of the bell?
5   What prevents learning taking place earlier? Do you have control over this? For example, is it because children arrive late from PE or is it because of the way in which you choose to start your lesson?
6   Do you start your lesson by collecting or handing back homework? Do you have to? Could you do this in the middle of a lesson, perhaps as a break between two learning activities?

Consider the last ten minutes of *your* lessons:
1   Do you summarize and reinforce what has been learned?
2   Do you do this consciously and consistently?
3   Is this a systematic review, involving all students?
4   Are students actively involved in the review?
5   Is the review at the end of each lesson part of a wider, systematic review?
6   Do you spend the last few minutes of a lesson issuing homework? Do you have to? Could you give out homework in the middle of the lesson, perhaps as a break between two learning activities?

Are you fully exploiting the opportunities to learn and to review learning at the beginnings and ends of your lessons?

- How long does your introduction last for?

- How would your students answer this question?

- How long is it really?

Teachers often underestimate how long they talk for, particularly at the beginning of the lesson.

- Keep a stopwatch and time your introductions for few weeks, or be observed and receive some feedback.

- Aim to keep your introduction to a maximum of ten minutes. Set an alarm clock – if you are still talking after ten minutes, shut up!

- Try to break up lessons into a series of shorter activities. Long activities can be broken up by giving back or setting homework or by allowing students a two minute 'state break'.

4 Activities often last longer than students' concentration spans

Teachers often underestimate how long they talk for. Almost without exception, teachers are comfortable when talking to a class of students, and proficient at it – it is something that they do every day. Walk around any school when lessons are in progress and more often than not you will see teachers standing at the front of the room talking. Ask them how long they talked for in their lessons and invariably they will underestimate, often quite considerably.

Often, teachers begin the lesson by standing at the front talking. They may be recapping on the previous lesson or introducing the new one. Sometimes, they will involve students by asking a series of questions, while on other occasions they will explain a new idea or concept themselves. It is a typical classroom activity and one enacted in countless classrooms on a daily basis.

In many respects, whole-class activities involving the teacher explaining, questioning or conducting a class discussion have always been the 'bread and butter' of classroom life. I offer no criticism of such activities, other than to observe that their lengths often exceed the students' concentration spans. Most children have a concentration span around two minutes longer than their chronological age in minutes; for some, it is considerably less. This means that Year 7 students will begin to lose concentration after around 13 minutes of a learning activity, while even the oldest students in secondary schools – and this includes adults – cannot concentrate for longer than 20–25 minutes (see page 35).

However, *I frequently observe lesson activities, including the teacher-led introduction, lasting for 30 minutes or more.* While some activities allow individuals to take a mental break when they need one, without disturbing other people, this is not always possible in a whole-class situation.

Implications for learning

- Children cannot help but lose concentration if they are engaged in an activity for over 20 minutes without a short mental break. When activities, especially the introduction, last longer than 20 minutes, learning will be dramatically impaired.

- The beginning of a lesson is often spent recapping on the previous lesson and introducing the new topic. By the time the teacher has got on to teaching the new material, no one is listening!

- When children are engaged in the same activity for too long, they get bored. When they become bored at the beginning of the lesson, it is very hard to regain their interest later on.

- Children who are bored will become restless and potentially disruptive. Many discipline problems stem from bored students.

- How many learning activities do you normally employ during a lesson?

- Do you tend to employ the same, or similar, activities on a regular basis?

- Do your lessons tend to follow a set pattern? Is it similar to the one outlined opposite?

- Do you consciously seek to employ a range of strategies in every lesson?

Seek to create lots of 'beginnings' in your lessons – keep the 'middle' to a minimum.

Learning will be enhanced if you employ a range of shorter and varied activities in your lessons.

5 Lessons often consist of a single learning activity

Many lessons follow the same basic pattern, and consist of:

- an *introduction* to the whole class, often involving questions and answers
- an *explanation* by the teacher of the new material
- an *activity* lasting for approximately 30 minutes involving individuals in comprehension or note-making exercises based on textbook, worksheet or blackboard
- a brief *summing up*
- the setting of *homework.*

Lessons that consist of two, three or even four very different activities are scarce and often confined to modern language lessons, which are a notable exception to this generalization. It is much more likely that an explanation by the teacher will be followed by a single main learning activity.

Often, this activity will follow a similar pattern from lesson to lesson, as all teachers have their preferred teaching style and have a small number of learning strategies that they rely heavily upon and employ on a regular basis. I make no value judgement regarding the relative merits of various strategies, but simply point out that most teachers employ a narrow range of strategies in the classroom, which reflect their preferred style.

Implications for learning

- The main learning activity often lasts for around 30 minutes. This is in excess of students' concentration spans and can easily lead to them becoming bored.

- Whatever the nature of the activity, around two-thirds of students will be disadvantaged as they will not be working in their preferred learning style (see page 41).

- As teachers tend to work within a narrow range of strategies, it is often the same two-thirds of the class who are being required to work outside their preferred style, from lesson to lesson.

- Students often cover each learning point only once. By limiting lessons to one main activity the chances of applying new knowledge and covering the same concepts in different ways are greatly reduced.

- Lessons that consist of only one main activity have one beginning and lots of 'middle'. Students learn more at the beginning of a learning experience (see page 37) and so learning can be enhanced by employing a number of activities during the course of a lesson, in order to create several 'beginnings'.

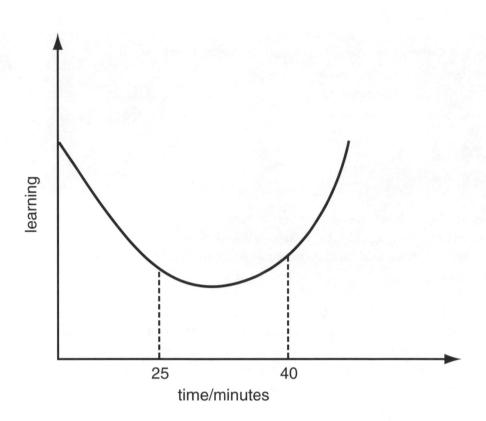

Key learning points are often covered between 25 and 40 minutes into a lesson.

This is precisely the time when the capacity to learn and remember is at its lowest.

Key learning points should be:

- introduced at the beginning of the lesson

- developed, consolidated and applied during the lesson

- reviewed and reinforced at the end of the lesson.

6 The key learning point is often delivered in the middle of the lesson

The key learning point is the *most important* part of the lesson. For example:

> *'Volcanoes are located near plate boundaries.'*
>
> *'Do the calculation in brackets first.'*
>
> *'Keep the wrist firm when playing a volley.'*

The key learning point is the piece of information, knowledge, concept or 'law' that everyone must grasp, and, quite probably, the bit that needs to be understood before further progress can be made in a particular topic. *It is the bit you would cover if the lesson lasted for only two minutes.*

The timing of the delivery of the key learning point is significant. We know that learners remember more from the beginning of a learning experience and that a student's capacity to learn is greatest at the start of a lesson (page 37) – however, in practice, students often encounter the key learning point between 25 and 40 minutes into a lesson.

It can be claimed, with some justification, that not all lessons have a key moment – for example, a GCSE art lesson where the group is engaged in an ongoing piece of coursework. It is also true that, in certain situations, the key learning point of the lesson will be different for individual students. However, the vast majority of lessons will, or at least should, contain a key learning point and the timing of its delivery is of considerable importance.

Implications for learning
- If the key learning point is introduced between 25 and 40 minutes into a lesson, the chances of it being understood and remembered are greatly reduced as the middle of the lesson is precisely the time when a students capacity to learn and remember is at its lowest!

- This is compounded if the first 25 minutes have consisted of a teacher led introduction. The key learning point is introduced just as the students are beginning to lose concentration.

Reflect on your own lessons:

- **When do you think you usually deliver the key learning point during a lesson?**

- **Do you start with it?**

- **Are you always *aware* of the key learning point you wish to cover in a lesson?**

Make enough copies of the graph opposite for every lesson that you will teach for the next fortnight. Identify the time at which you cover the key learning point in each lesson and plot it on a copy of the graph.

- **Is there a pattern?**

- **When is the key moment in most of your lessons – at the beginning or in the middle?**

How predictable are your lessons?

- How predictable are your lessons in terms of the format you use?

- How predictable are your lessons in terms of the learning activities you use?

- How many of the questions opposite could your students accurately answer about your lessons?

What could you change to make your lessons less predictable?

- the layout of the room?

- the wall displays?

- the format of the lesson?

- the learning activities?

7 Lessons are often highly predictable

Ask any students what they will be doing in their next English, maths or geography lesson and they will usually have a good idea. They will not necessarily know what the subject matter will be, but they will often be able to predict with considerable accuracy the form that the lesson will take.

For any teacher – including you – students will be able to predict some, if not most, of the following:

1   Will the teacher be waiting outside the classroom or will he or she arrive after the students?

2   How will the furniture in the classroom be organized?

3   What will be on the walls?

4   How will the lesson start?

5   Will the teacher start by taking the register?

6   Will the teacher ask some questions about the last lesson?

7   Who will the teacher probably ask?

8   Will the teacher talk for a long time at the start of the lesson?

9   Will you have to do much writing?

10   Will you use a textbook? Can you guess which one?

11   Will you be allowed, or even encouraged, to talk to other students about your work?

12   Will you be required to work as part of a group?

13   Will you have to stand up and move around the room during the lesson?

14   Will you have to find out information for yourself?

15   Will you use computers? If so, what for?

16   Will homework be set at the beginning, in the middle or at the end of the lesson?

Most teachers have a preferred teaching style and have developed an approach to lessons that they are comfortable with and consider effective. Not only do lessons tend to follow a similar basic pattern, but teachers also frequently employ the same or similar learning activities. Even teachers who consider themselves 'different' from their colleagues are often predictably so.

Implications for learning
Learning, concentration and memory are significantly enhanced when students encounter situations that are unusual and unexpected (see page 49). When students come across something different, particularly at the beginning of the lesson, the sense of anticipation and slight release of adrenaline greatly contributes to the learning process.

The predictability of many lessons, both in format and activity, fails to activate the heightened sensory awareness and sense of curiosity associated with novelty, and acts as an artificial limit on learning.

When students are placed under negative stress, it is inevitable that no learning will take place and highly likely that they will become restless and disruptive.

8 Students are often placed under negative stress

I hated maths lessons as a child. In particular, I hated the thought of being asked a question that I couldn't answer (and that was most of them) and looking foolish in front of the rest of the class. I did all that I could to avoid having to answer a question; I carefully avoided eye contact with the teacher, never sat on the end of a row in case each student was to be asked a question in turn and did all that I could to remain inconspicuous. By concentrating really hard and taking every available precaution, I became something of an expert in survival. Unfortunately, I learned very little during maths lessons and, although very successful at avoiding questions, I was simultaneously and spectacularly unsuccessful at mathematics.

I am still an expert in survival, as indeed all of us are. (I never sit by the flipchart during INSET sessions for fear of embarrassing myself by making a ludicrous spelling error.) Children in particular are adept at surviving during lessons, even if it means being disruptive to do so. Every time we teach a lesson, in a subject that makes perfect sense to us, there are children who are hating every minute, living in dread of being made to look foolish in front of their friends. However kind and compassionate the teacher is and however hard they have striven to create a climate of trust in which all students are respected, there will be children suffering from various degrees of stress.

Teachers do not intend to place students under stress, although experienced teachers can easily do so if and when required. Teachers are trying to create an atmosphere of control and a sense of challenge in their lessons. However, it is a fine line between challenge and stress and it is drawn in a different place for each individual student. Consequently, many of our daily classroom practices unintentionally create precisely the stressful environment for some that acts as a barrier to learning. For example:

- *Being asked a question.* This often happens at the beginning of a lesson. By persisting with a student who is unable or unwilling to answer a question, we are driving the student deeper into survival mode, making it increasingly unlikely that he or she will answer correctly, despite all the 'help' we think we are giving. Indeed, it is highly doubtful that they are thinking about the question at all.

- *Having to read out loud.* The thought of stuttering or mispronouncing a word makes the chances of stuttering or mispronunciation even more likely!

- *The word 'test'.* If there is one word designed to prevent students doing justice to their ability, it is the word 'test'. When a target of seven out of ten correct answers is thrown in for good measure, the feeling of stress is greatly intensified.

- *Any task that is not fully understood.* Nothing creates stress like the fear of failure. For some students, every day is a succession of tasks that they cannot, or at least *believe* they cannot, complete successfully. School is little more than an ordeal and the chance of any learning taking place is just about nil.

'Lessons should be hard to forget.'

Year 8 student

9 Most lessons are forgotten within 24 hours

A few years ago, I was conducting some research into what makes a good lesson from the student's perspective. *'Lessons should be hard to forget'*, was the perceptive and highly memorable reply from a Year 8 boy. He was too polite to add that many, however, are far from memorable; on the contrary, many lessons are instantly forgettable. Not only do students often find it difficult to recall the subject content of previous lessons, many *teachers*, without reference to a diary or planner, find it difficult to remember what they covered the last time they taught any particular group. The fact that 'forgetting' on such a dramatic scale takes place even if the last lesson was only yesterday only adds to the frustration.

Our frustration is understandable, but we should not be surprised at the extent of our 'forgetting', as it is well established that, without systematic review, over 80 per cent of information is 'lost' within 24 hours (page 53). The only surprise is that the frustration that all teachers have felt on occasions has not evolved into a determination to ensure that students remember much more of their lessons. For teaching lessons only for them to be forgotten a day later is more than frustrating; it is futile and has some extremely damaging consequences for the learning process.

Not only do lessons begin with frustrated teachers and students being 'told' that they have 'failed' because they cannot remember the last lesson, *significant amounts of time are wasted by the necessity to 're-teach'* material. There is a subtle, but significant difference between spending time at the beginning of a lesson reviewing and reinforcing previously learned material, and teaching a topic again, effectively from scratch.

Reviewing material is a conscious and effective strategy designed to cement learning; re-teaching is nothing more than a waste of time. By the time the previous lesson has been hurriedly re-taught and we are ready to move on to 'today's lesson', we are 30 minutes into the session and the students' concentration spans have expired. What is more, its a certain guarantee that the next lesson will be condemned to exactly the same format!

If lessons should indeed be 'hard to forget', we need to be clear about what we can do in the classroom to make our lessons memorable. Similarly, we need to analyse the reasons why *so much is forgotten, so quickly, by so many* and, rather than accept it as one of the job's inevitable frustrations, we must do something about it.

Exploring the reasons *why* students find it so difficult to remember their lessons is an exercise rarely undertaken by teachers, either collectively or individually and yet it is a necessary and important step in order to ensure that increased amounts of information are remembered in the future. If we are aware of *why* students forget, we can attempt to do something about it.

On page 115 are four common reasons why so much information is forgotten so quickly.

To what extent do they apply to your lessons?

Improve recall by:

- emphasizing context – actively engage the student

- identifying the key learning point of a lesson or unit of work – teach it in a dramatic, unusual and unexpected way

- developing understanding

- encouraging students to systematically review their work.

1 *Lessons that are heavily dependent upon content memory are easily forgotten.* These are the lessons in which the emphasis is on the transfer of information from the teacher to the student. They often involve a large amount of note-taking, punctuated by an explanation from the teacher or a flurry of questions and answers, and/or comprehension exercises.

These lessons are forgotten so quickly because students have not been actively engaged in their learning: there is very little 'doing'. We know that the brain remembers context much better than it remembers content (see page 49) yet these lessons are largely 'context free zones' making them unlikely to be recalled.

2 *Lessons that are boring and mundane are easily forgotten.* The brain best remembers anything that is unusual, exaggerated or unexpected. The next time you discover that an entire class has forgotten the contents of a lesson, reflect on the extent to which it had been a dramatic and 'different' experience for them.

An effective strategy to significantly improve recall is to make your lessons unusual so as to increase the sense of anticipation, curiosity and concentration. Of course, it is not always possible to make every lesson different; identify the key learning points of a lesson or unit of work and make a conscious effort to deliver them in a dramatic and unexpected way. Discuss ideas for such strategies in subject teams and write them into schemes of work.

3 *Lessons that are not understood will be quickly forgotten.* Although understanding and memory are two separate things, the chances of material being recalled are significantly greater when it has been understood. Consider the subjects in which you struggled at school; the chances are that these were the subjects you found difficult to understand.

Lessons that are heavy in content often emphasize the transfer of information, at the expense of understanding. For students to understand something they must be fully engaged with it, thinking about it, applying it and making personal sense out of it. Failure to develop understanding will inevitably result in the lesson being quickly forgotten.

4 *Information that is not systematically reviewed will inevitably be quickly forgotten.* Students who rush out of a classroom at the end of a lesson, and next think about the subject matter at the beginning of the following session, have very little chance of recalling anything substantial.

For material to be remembered it must be reviewed (see page 53) and it must be reviewed systematically. It need not be time consuming, but the exercise of identifying and reviewing the key points at the end of a lesson is a small time investment that will yield considerable dividends. When students get into the habit of reviewing their key points again after 24 hours, and again a week after the learning activity, recall will be dramatically improved. Try it and see!

Nearly 90 per cent of students respond to the word association prompt 'lessons' with the reply:

BORING!

10   Students are often bored

There will be those who feel that my claim that 'students are often bored' is overstating the case. Maybe it is, but if I am guilty of exaggeration, it is only slight, for there is evidence all around of bored secondary school students. Certainly students are sometimes bored in *my* lessons – not always, I hope, and not all of them at the same time, but certainly it is a factor that, as a teacher, I would be foolish to ignore.

For nearly a decade now, I have employed a word association exercise with every new group of students that I have worked with. It is an extremely large sample that includes students of all ages and abilities, from very different schools in a variety of geographical areas. Very nearly 90 per cent of them have responded to the prompt *'lessons'* with the reply, *'BORING'*. While accepting that the exercise lacks a degree of 'rigour' in terms of academic research, and that many teenagers may feel *obliged* to offer such a reply, I find the sheer consistency of the response of interest, if nothing else.

Of further significance is the unanimous agreement among teachers that students learn most effectively when they are interested in their work and enjoy what they are doing. I sometimes refer to it as the '**O** Factor' as it is the difference between children coming to school saying, '*Oh good, it's maths today*' and '*Oh God, it's maths today*'. With the former, the battle is half won, while with the latter, it is almost certainly lost.

If capturing students' interest in the lesson is so significant, not to mention difficult, it is extraordinary that teachers collectively devote so little time to considering how their lessons could be made more interesting. Why is it that students find Mr Smith's lessons so interesting? How does one teacher in the faculty manage to maintain a high degree of interest in her lessons even when covering a particularly dry part of the syllabus that students in other classes find boring? When was the last time you sat down as a team of teachers and discussed this issue? Almost all teachers accept the desirability of keeping students interested in their work, but few have ever considered how.

Certainly, there are teachers who, through their sheer personality, manage to keep the boredom factor at bay, while those who can deliver a barrage of jokes while simultaneously juggling with their feet do have something of an advantage when it comes to entertaining. Yet capturing and sustaining interest in a lesson is not simply due to an inherent ability to entertain, which teachers were supposed to be born with. Ultimately, it is the lesson and the learning activities that children have to find interesting if they are going to learn effectively, and strategies to try to make them interesting can most certainly be discussed and shared among colleagues.

Boredom is not inevitable – it is not simply a symptom of the teen years or a product of puberty. The key is to find the reason *why* students are bored and do something about it.

> **On page 119 is a list of some common reasons for boredom, all of which the teacher has at least some control over.**
>
> ***To what extent do they apply to your lessons?***

When students are bored they will almost certainly become restless and many will eventually become disruptive.

1   *Students are not engaged in the lesson*. These are the lessons in which students are the passive recipients of information. They take a lot of notes and/or complete low level comprehension exercises. There is very little 'doing' going on. *'All we ever do is copy off the board.'*

2   *Lessons are predictable*. Students know the form that the lesson will take and have a good idea what they will be required to do. There is little variation in the types of tasks that are set and the activities in the lesson are selected from a very narrow range of styles. *'We always use the same textbook.'*

3   *Activities last too long*. When students are engaged in activities that last longer than their concentration spans, they will eventually become bored and their attention will wander. When a lesson consists of only one activity, there is a danger that students will be engaged on the same task for too long.

4   *Teacher talks too much*. Teachers are good at talking and often underestimate how long they talk for, particularly at the beginning of the lesson. When the teacher talks for longer than ten minutes, students will get bored. Lessons with a large amount of 'teacher talk' are often low on 'doing' and fail to fully engage the class. *'All he ever does is talk.'*

5   *Students are regularly required to work outside of their preferred learning style*. It is little wonder that kinesthetic learners (see page 41) become bored if all they are asked to do is sit and write. Think of the three students that always appear bored in your lessons – the chances are they are kinesthetic learners. *'I hate writing.'*

6   *Students don't understand the work they are doing*. Anybody – child or adult – will quickly become switched off if they are involved in activities that they do not understand. The fact that students can still successfully complete what are little more than low level comprehension exercises should not be allowed to disguise their lack of genuine understanding.

7   *The work is too easy*. Sadly, this is a factor that can easily affect bright students and is the result of work that fails to stretch them and build on what they already know. It is common in, but not exclusive to, Years 7 and 8 when, despite the National Curriculum, teachers often need, or certainly feel the need, to cover material that the student has encountered before. This is exacerbated in subjects that the student particularly enjoys, as they will almost certainly have read around the subject or watched relevant television programmes at home.

8   *The work is too hard*. Anybody will get bored when they cannot cope with the tasks that have been set. Few people find failure much fun, particularly consistent failure.

9   *The activities lack challenge*. Irrespective of the subject matter, children respond to a challenge. When activities are mundane and routine they are highly unlikely to capture the imagination and are almost certainly recipes for boredom.

Shut your eyes: picture one of your lessons. Make your picture as real as possible. Include as much detail as you can. Start from the time the students enter the classroom and work your way through to the end of the lesson. Try to involve all five senses.

Identify any features of the lesson that help children to learn. Conversely, identify any features that either hinder learning or fail to promote it.

In what ways does this picture differ from the one that you 'painted' on page 64?

The answer to this question gives you a clue to your Learning Gap.

YOUR CLASSROOM

The points made in the preceding pages are observations rather than criticisms. They are also generalizations, which may or may not apply to your lessons.

They are intended to make teachers think carefully about both what they frequently do in the classroom and why they do it. Establishing a clear picture of your current practice is a necessary and important step in establishing your personal Learning Gap. It is something that you cannot do alone; you are simply too close to it. While self-reflection is a worthwhile and potentially powerful exercise, it needs to be reinforced by objective independent information, generated by observation.

Self-reflection, however, is a useful starting point – it is ongoing, highly personal and it can be done in the relative safety of isolation. No one need ever know the outcome.

> **Reflect on the ten features of current practice detailed in this section and listed again below.**
>
> **To what extent do they apply to *your* lessons?**

		Frequently	Occasionally	Never
1	Students spend the majority of their time reading, writing and listening.			
2	Students answer a lot of questions.			
3	The beginnings and ends of lessons are often wasted.			
4	Activities – especially the introduction by the teacher – often last longer than the students' concentration spans.			
5	Many lessons consist of a single main activity.			
6	The key learning point is often delivered in the middle of the lesson.			
7	Lessons are highly predictable.			
8	Students are often placed under negative stress.			
9	Most lessons are forgotten within 24 hours.			
10	Students are often bored.			

Your Learning Gap:

- is highly personal

- will constantly change

- will be different for various groups

- will be different for individual students

- will be different on a Tuesday morning to on a Friday afternoon.

YOUR LEARNING GAP

The Learning Gap is the difference between what we know about effective learning and what is currently happening in the classroom. More accurately, as far as you are concerned, it is the difference between effective learning and what is happening in *your* classroom. For the Learning Gap is highly personal and will vary significantly from teacher to teacher. Identifying it and implementing strategies to close it is the way in which teachers can make their classroom practice more effective, and is therefore the key to significant, genuine and sustained school improvement.

All teachers, however experienced and effective, have a Learning Gap; only when it is accepted that this is not a personal criticism, but a professional development agenda, can progress be made, both individually and collectively. In many cases, the gap has not been created by any serious weaknesses in classroom practice, but is the result of the rapid and dramatic advances in our understanding of how the brain works and how we learn. Consequently, it is a gap that can never be considered to be permanently closed; each time that new information becomes available, we have to reassess it and respond to it.

Although I would suggest that a Learning Gap exists in all classrooms, this does not imply that I believe the gap is necessarily a particularly large one. It is easy and understandable for teachers to assume that any comment upon their teaching must be a condemnation, and a judgement that their current practice is somehow unsatisfactory. However, for many teachers the difference between how people learn effectively and what happens in their classrooms may be little more than a cavity; but, as with any cavity, it needs filling.

In OFSTED-speak, the issue is not simply about improving the quality of the small amount of *unsatisfactory* teaching that occurs in schools. Rather, our challenge is to help teachers turn *satisfactory* and *good* lessons into *very good* and *excellent* ones. By applying some polish in the right places and improving our performance by just 5 per cent we can make a significant difference to the way in which students learn. By closing our Learning Gap – be it cavity or chasm – we are making progress and unlocking a little more of the amazing learning potential of all our students.

In establishing the size and scope of our personal Learning Gap, it is important to remember that we are dealing with an issue that is in a *constant state of flux*. The way in which we approach teaching a top set Year 8 class on a Tuesday morning is likely to be very different from the way in which we deal with a Year 10 lower set on a Friday afternoon. Some of these differences will be conscious strategies, which may or may not be legitimate and effective. On other occasions, teachers may be oblivious to the different way in which they treat various groups. For example, the teacher who greets her favourite Year 7 group with a smile and a welcoming word can easily be the same person who avoids eye contact with the bottom set that she dreads, as she scowls a warning that they had better behave this lesson, or else!

To what extent do you – as an individual teacher, as a faculty and as a school – have control over the following?

- what you teach
- how you teach it
- the length of lessons
- the structure of the school day
- the length of learning activities
- the way in which you start your lessons
- the physical and emotional state in which students arrive at your lessons
- the way you respond to the physical and emotional state of your students
- the physical appearance of your classroom
- what you say
- what you do
- your smile!

Not only are teachers often unaware of the different messages they give their groups, both verbally and through their body language, they are also unaware of the impact that these messages have upon the way in which their various students behave and learn. There is much evidence to suggest that a powerful and effective strategy to improve learning is to approach the group that you dread teaching as if they were your favourite class.

It may well be worthwhile, therefore, to think not in terms of your *single* Learning Gap, but of a Learning Gap for each *group*, or even for every *individual* that you teach.

There are, of course, a number of factors that contribute to the Learning Gap, some of which *teachers have little or no control over*. Teachers have no control over the curriculum they are required to teach; a crowded, content-based and (some would argue) inappropriate curriculum. Nor have they any control over the limited and restrictive way in which society measures learning and intelligence through the public examination system. Closer to home, they have little control over whole-school policies and practices, some of which fail to encourage effective learning as much as they might, or over the emotional and physical state in which students arrive at school.

Teachers do, however, have control over their own classrooms and therefore exert a degree of influence over issues that initially might appear to be outside of their direct control. The curriculum may be imposed upon us, but we are free to interpret and teach it in the way in which we feel most appropriate. Similarly, the fact that a particular student arrives at a lesson in an unhelpful emotional state, because of circumstances at home, does not mean that we cannot recognize the signals and respond appropriately. We may have no control over the student's home background, but we do have total control over the way in which our actions contribute to and affect his or her state of mind.

There are aspects of the Learning Gap over which teachers, as individuals, may feel they have little control, but there is much that can be done collectively, as a faculty or as a whole school, to address these issues and enhance learning. The provision of breakfast bars and drinking fountains, the lengths of lessons, the timing and lengths of breaks, the way in which teachers are disturbed during lessons, the way students are grouped, the deployment of staff, schemes of work, meeting schedules, staff development ... the list goes on.

Closing the Learning Gap therefore requires an individual and a collective response at a variety of levels. For individual teachers, there is much that can be done immediately in their own classrooms, even in areas over which they may initially consider themselves to have no control. For the faculty and whole-school manager, a consideration of the Learning Gap is required on a different scale, if policy and organization are to enable all students to maximize their learning potential.

Establishing your Learning Gap – a summary

A INTERESTING THINGS ABOUT LEARNING	B IMPLICATIONS FOR THE CLASSROOM	C CURRENT SITUATION IN MANY CLASSROOMS	D YOUR LESSONS	E YOUR GAP (DIFFERENCE BETWEEN B AND D)	F HOW COULD YOU CLOSE THE GAP?
We only use around two per cent of our brainpower.	Students are capable of learning much more than many teachers believe.	Many children significantly underperform in the classroom.			
The brain needs oxygen, water and rest to function efficiently.	More oxygen would get to the brain if children were required to stand up and move around in lessons.	Children spend large amounts of lessons sitting down. The brain becomes increasingly inefficient.			
People do not learn when placed under negative stress.	'Low stress–high challenge' is the optimum for learning.	Questions and tests are all sources of negative stress.			
Concentration span is approximately two minutes in excess of chronological age.	Learning should be broken into chunks of around 15 minutes or less.	Many activities – particularly teacher introductions – last far in excess of students' maximum concentration spans.			
People learn more at the beginning of a learning experience (BEM principle).	Lessons should have lots of 'beginnings'. Make the most of the beginning of the lesson.	Most lessons consist of an introduction and one main activity. This means there is a lot of 'middle'. The optimum time for learning at the beginning of the lesson is often wasted.			

A INTERESTING THINGS ABOUT LEARNING	B IMPLICATIONS FOR THE CLASSROOM	C CURRENT SITUATION IN MANY CLASSROOMS	D YOUR LESSONS	E YOUR GAP (DIFFERENCE BETWEEN B AND D)	F HOW COULD YOU CLOSE THE GAP?
People learn best in different ways.	Each lesson should include a variety of activities to cater for visual, auditory and, in particular, kinesthetic learners.	Children spend a large amount of time reading, writing and listening. Kinesthetic learners are often neglected. In many cases, these students become restless and even disruptive.			
Learning is greatly enhanced when the whole brain is engaged.	Learners need to see the Big Picture first (jigsaw box) before encountering the detail (jigsaw pieces). Lessons should include activities that connect the two hemispheres of the brain.	Children spend a large amount of time reading, writing and listening. These are predominantly left-brain activities.			
People remember context better than content.	Place learning experiences in a context. Make sure the learner has to 'do' something.	Children are expected to learn large amounts of content by rote. Writing notes to learn is a common activity. There is too much content and not enough context.			

A INTERESTING THINGS ABOUT LEARNING	B IMPLICATIONS FOR THE CLASSROOM	C CURRENT SITUATION IN MANY CLASSROOMS	D YOUR LESSONS	E YOUR GAP (DIFFERENCE BETWEEN B AND D)	F HOW COULD YOU CLOSE THE GAP?
People remember dramatic, unusual and emotional experiences.	Learning experiences should engage the emotions. Look for different, unusual ways of presenting key information. Make use of the exaggerated and the absurd.	Learning experiences are often highly predictable and lessons often follow the same pattern. Many learning activities are mundane – even boring.			
Regular review dramatically improves recall. Without review, information is forgotten almost immediately.	Spend the last ten minutes of the lesson identifying and reviewing the key points. Encourage students to review their work at home. Start the lesson by reviewing previous work.	The end of the lesson is often wasted. Children are rarely required to systematically review their work.			
People learn best when they want to learn. Motivation is therefore very important for effective learning.	Allow students to feel they have some control over their learning, and make lessons enjoyable. Help students succeed and give them a feeling of hope.	Students are often bored and 'switch off' during lessons, particularly when they feel they are failing.			

My personal Learning Gap

Use this table to reflect on your own practice and what you could do to improve learning in your classroom.

	Issue	Strategy to 'close the gap'
1		
2		
3		
4		
5		

A key task is to ensure that the recent advances in our understanding of how we learn are translated into lesson activities.

Section Three

Closing the Learning Gap

This section aims to offer a range of practical strategies that are designed to help develop the quality of teaching across an institution.

Closing the Learning Gap demands an individual and a collective response. If the challenge for individual teachers is to incorporate into their teaching strategies that will close their personal Learning Gap, the challenge for the school is somewhat different. School managers have both to create a climate in which teachers want to improve and develop their practice, and to provide the encouragement and support that is required for it to be done successfully.

Individuals, however well meaning, will invariably enjoy only limited success working alone. Closing the Learning Gap involves teachers engaging in a *reflection-observation-feedback loop*, which has significantly more chance of succeeding when teams of teachers begin the process simultaneously. If nothing else, the mutual support afforded by working as part of a team reduces the morale-sapping sense of isolation that is a potential consequence of teachers embarking on this journey alone, and can often encourage colleagues both to begin and to continue the process of professional development.

Although an institutional approach that attempts to improve the quality of learning at a variety of levels is desirable, the highly individual nature of the Learning Gap prevents a blanket response to closing it. All teachers will identify different areas of their performance that, if modified, would lead to enhanced learning in their lessons, ensuring that an individual response is required. In many cases, having identified the issue, the response is self-evident: teachers who recognize that they often talk for 35 minutes at the start of the lesson, need to make a conscious effort to reduce the amount of talking they do, limiting their introductions to a maximum of ten minutes.

WHOLE-SCHOOL STRATEGIES FOR CLOSING THE GAP

The aim is to create opportunities for teachers to turn their attention increasingly to the core business of schools – *helping our students learn.* A central plank of any strategy is likely to be the creation of opportunities for teachers to observe each other in action and so benefit from the considerable expertise that exists within any institution. A greater challenge for whole-school managers is to develop a climate in which teachers will be encouraged not only to recognize these opportunities, but also to fully exploit them.

As with any mammoth undertaking, it is worthwhile dividing the challenge, at least in the mind, into smaller chunks. Developing the quality of teaching in a school requires consideration of two separate, but related, key issues:

1   logistical and organizational matters
2   people.

I am here to help children learn.

I do this by...

More specifically, any strategy must take into account the two issues that teachers identify as being the barriers to the widespread development of classroom practice:

1 the implied criticism of their current practice
2 a lack of time.

We are therefore trying to find time, or rather the money that will generate time, for teachers to be *able* to develop their practice, while insulating the whole initiative with sufficient reassurance so that they will *want* to.

School managers have been managing change for a decade or more and are well aware of the potential reaction of colleagues when they are faced with such sensitive and potentially threatening developments. Consequently, it is not the intention of this book to try and tell experienced school leaders how to handle their staff. Rather, this section aims to offer a range of *practical strategies that are designed to develop the quality of teaching across an institution.*

All of the strategies described below are currently being used, with success, in secondary schools in various parts of the UK. With the exception of the first point, they are in no particular order. They are not the 'right answer', nor do they guarantee success. They are simply suggestions that can be adopted or adapted as required. If nothing else, they raise a number of relevant issues and may help focus the thoughts of anyone charged with the responsibility of developing teaching quality in a school.

Involvement of the headteacher

The leadership and active involvement of the headteacher is crucial. If the core activity in a school is learning, and the key to a school's success is what goes on in its classrooms, there is a strong argument that the headteacher should spend a substantial proportion of his or her working week in and around lessons.

Making it The Priority

Developing the quality of teaching has to be an identified priority. Not only has it to be an identified priority, it has to be accepted as such by all. As *The* Priority, in fact, it must underpin whole-school strategic planning and inform all key decisions. It also demands that sufficient resources are made available for progress to be made. If you can't *find* the money for it, is it *really* your priority?

Rewriting the job descriptions

Rewrite the job descriptions of all staff: Headteacher, classroom teachers and support staff. Replace each existing version with one based on this template:

I AM HERE TO HELP CHILDREN LEARN.
I do this by ...

Deciding who is responsible

Whose responsibility is it to develop the quality of classroom practice? To be successful, such a project requires an extraordinary amount of time and energy and yet all too often it is a responsibility handed to a senior member of staff who also has numerous other demanding whole-school tasks to carry out.

'The biggest and most underused resource teachers have is each other.'

Learning and Teaching Scotland

Alternatives for allocating responsibility for developing classroom practice include:

1   *Make it the sole responsibility of a member of the senior team*. If done well, it will be more than worth the investment. It is a 24-hours-a-day, seven-days-a-week challenge that *cannot* be met if energy is dissipated among numerous management and administrative tasks.

2   *Make it the responsibility of the headteacher* and significantly reduce his or her other commitments, by delegating administrative tasks, to enable the development to be carried out effectively. It is a powerful message that there is *nothing* more important in a school than what goes on in classrooms.

3   *Make it the prime responsibility of all members of the senior team*. If it is the whole-school priority, it is important that all management decisions and actions are informed and underpinned by a collective desire to enhance learning. It can be argued that the task requires such an enormous time and energy commitment, that it *cannot* be made the responsibility of one individual.

4   *Make it the responsibility of a member of staff outside the senior team*. This can reduce the sense of threat and feeling of accountability that can all too easily accompany initiatives to improve the teaching quality that are driven from above. Suspicion can be greatly reduced if the perception is that 'This is controlled by teachers for the benefit of teachers'.

5   *Heads of Faculty or Department* have a leading role to play in developing the quality of learning in their particular subject. Their role has evolved considerably from simply ordering the stationery, and must surely revolve around helping children to learn. It is all too easy for Heads of Faculty to adopt a limited monitoring role, checking that homework is set because it is Wednesday or that exercise books have been marked. In many respects the middle management tier is the key to a successful school and, to this end, the active involvement of Heads of Faculty in the development and evaluation of learning is vital. Consider your Heads of Faculty and other key middle managers; what do you consider are their current ratios of monitoring work to development work?

Recognizing and disseminating good practice

A major challenge for those charged with the responsibility of improving classroom practice, and so enhancing the quality of learning in a school, is to both recognize and disseminate good practice. This can be done at a variety of levels: within the faculty, within the school and – if the artificially created competition between schools has not resulted in the drawbridge being raised – between neighbouring institutions.

All schools have excellent teachers. More specifically, all schools have teachers who are wonderful exponents of particular aspects of classroom practice, whose expertise could and should be shared with others. Some have developed a range of strategies to meet the needs of kinesthetic learners; others are skilful managers of group-work tasks; while others are notable for the unusual and dramatic way in which they start their lessons.

Labelling teachers as 'good' is imprecise. We need to be clear about *what* makes them so effective. Similarly, creating opportunities for teachers to observe each other at work in a general way will have only a limited effect. The key is to expose teachers to colleagues with *different* strengths who have been identified as possessing the specific skills that will help individual teachers close their personal Learning Gap.

All schools have excellent teachers.

More specifically, all schools have teachers who are wonderful exponents of particular aspects of classroom practice, whose expertise could and should be shared with others.

Creating time

Time for observation

Disseminating good practice means that opportunities have to be created for teachers to observe each other in the classroom. The budget-driven high contact ratios in many schools, and the competing pressure of so many other tasks, lead teachers to view, justifiably, any non-contact periods as sacrosanct. Although a small minority of teachers may choose to give up a precious non-contact period in order to visit a colleague's classroom, it is extremely unlikely that reliance on non-contact periods as the sole strategy will lead to lasting and widespread developments.

To be successful, *time must be made available*, in addition to non-contact periods, for teachers to observe each other in action. Although any comprehensive programme of observation involves a considerable cost commitment, it is both necessary and justified, if indeed developing the quality of teaching is your priority. Available options include:

1   Provide two 'supply days' per year or per term for each faculty. Teachers can be released from their lessons, as appropriate.

2   Use the headteacher and other members of the senior team to cover lessons. The knock-on benefit is that members of the senior team are increasingly in the classroom and are a presence around the school. Covering a lesson in which students are sharing textbooks in groups of three is a potentially more powerful message than a Head of Faculty constantly moaning about a low capitation allowance!

3   Timetable an extra non-contact period a week for each faculty, to be used solely for development purposes.

4   Make use of opportunities to 'team-teach'.

5   Generate income to be used solely for disseminating good practice. Invite neighbouring schools to send one or two members of staff to any training sessions that you are running for a nominal fee (say, £50). Whole-staff INSET days are obvious examples of such training sessions, but – as suggested on page 139 – not the only opportunities for teachers from several schools to work together.

Not only does the 'host school' benefit by generating money that can then be used to enable teachers to observe good practice; 'visiting schools' also gain access to very cheap training. It is also a way in which schools can assess the quality of INSET providers before making a decision about employing them to work in their own school.

Will this meeting help make me a better teacher?

Will this meeting improve students' learning?

Structure

It is highly unlikely that teachers will take up the offer of being released from a teaching commitment to observe a colleague teach *unless someone is driving the programme*. Making the development of teaching quality the school's priority does not automatically mean that every teacher will see it as his or her own personal priority. Observation programmes tend to be more successful when they are structured and overseen by a senior member of staff. For example, the programme leader might direct all teachers to observe two lessons per term – one within the faculty and one from another subject. Without structure, observation is something that teachers may just not get around to arranging.

Time for feedback, reflection and planning

Creating time for classroom observation is only half the challenge. We must also find time for teachers to reflect upon events in their classrooms and to plan increasingly effective learning experiences for their students.

- *Create the necessary time by abandoning meetings*. Teachers should come out of meetings as potentially better teachers; if this is *not* the case, then why have them? As better teachers are able to help their students to learn more effectively, a useful rule of thumb to gauge whether a meeting is necessary or not is to consider its likely impact upon students' learning.

- *Keep administration to a minimum*. Use weekly bulletins and/or departmental notice boards to pass on necessary information. If you start the day with a staff briefing, make one morning a week a faculty briefing, so that items of administration can be explained and *briefly* discussed.

- *Replace the traditional, and largely unnecessary, departmental meeting*, with two types of meeting: training sessions and planning sessions.

Training sessions

Do away with meetings in favour of a comprehensive staff development programme. Provide high quality training opportunities one night (3.30–5.00 pm) each week to complement and reinforce the training that takes place on whole-staff INSET days. Such a training programme:

1   can place 'effective learning' at its heart;

2   is cost effective – there is no supply or travel cost involved;

3   can use a combination of in-house expertise and external trainers;

4   is an opportunity for teachers who have been out on an INSET course to feed back to a wider audience;

5   can involve the entire staff in its construction – training needs can, in part, be identified through the Learning Gap exercise;

6   can be partly funded by inviting neighbouring schools to participate – a much more comprehensive programme can be devised if a cluster of schools work collaboratively;

7   could be made voluntary; staff will attend if they perceive it to be worthwhile – the key is to provide *quality* training;

8   should provide practical ideas – teachers must feel *'This is something that will help me in my classroom tomorrow'*;

Depersonalize the issue:

'We are evaluating strategies – not people.'

Closing the Learning Gap

9   can be used for faculties to explore effective learning in their own subject areas –
    'The goal' (see *Section Two*) can be established in such sessions;

10 can be used by individuals to reflect upon their own practice, receive feedback and
    so on.

Planning sessions

Alternate training sessions with planning sessions.

1   *Use planning sessions for subject team discussion groups:*

> *'I'm starting the Romans with Year 8 next week, any ideas?'*
>
> *'My intermediate set is struggling with quadratic equations. If I explain what we've done so far, I'd appreciate any suggestions as to what I might try next.'*
>
> *'Does anyone else teach 9R? I'm really struggling to gain their attention. Does anyone have any strategies that might work with them?'*
>
> *'I tried this activity with Year 7 last week and it worked really well.'*
>
> *'I saw this article in a magazine; it's got some really good lesson ideas.'*
>
> *'I had a breakthrough with Sam last week; he responded really well to...'*

2   *Include suggested lesson activities on all schemes of work that are planned.* Plan in groups
    of three – one person is responsible for activities for visual learners, the second for
    activities for auditory learners, while a third considers activities for kinesthetic
    learners.

3   *Plan lessons for the following week or unit.* Work in groups of three (as above) to
    consider the needs of all learners. Try to ensure that teachers with different preferred
    teaching styles have opportunities to work together.

4   *Plan lessons with a teacher from another department.* Use your colleague to offer a
    student's eye view of the lesson. For example, *'I don't understand that; how do you
    know that it will melt?'* is a view that a subject expert could easily neglect.

5   *Plan a lesson for someone else to teach.* Observe the lesson being taught and discuss it
    afterwards. The feeling of threat and potential failure is reduced if neither teacher
    has sole responsibility for the lesson. This is a good way of isolating the *activities*,
    and evaluating how effectively *they* contributed to learning rather than the
    performance of the individual teacher. To a certain extent, it is like watching yourself
    teach.

6   *Depersonalize the issue.* Constantly emphasize that it is classroom *activities* that are
    being discussed and evaluated, *not teachers*. We are interested in, *'How effectively did
    that group-work activity help children to learn?'* not, *'How good a teacher is Mr Smith?'*

What have you learned today?

Closing the Learning Gap

Keeping a high profile

A major challenge for those with whole-school responsibility is to ensure that *'learning'* enjoys a high profile in the school. Staff should not only be reminded at every opportunity that the school's identified priority for development is classroom practice, they should also be made aware of developments in brain science, recent publications, new learning materials, and so on.

This is not always easy, however; it is amazing just how many things teachers can find to get in the way of learning. Suggestions for raising awareness and keeping 'learning' high profile include:

1   maintaining a well stocked library of up-to-date 'learning' books in the staffroom;

2   encouraging staff to recommend books and other publications, or at least particularly interesting and important passages from them, to colleagues;

3   dedicating part of the staff room notice board to learning issues – use it to publicize courses and new publications, and for displaying interesting articles and passages from books;

4   including an article, passage or appropriate quote on the back of the weekly staff bulletin;

5   issuing each member of staff with a *'Do not disturb, learning in progress'* notice to put on the door during lessons;

6   displaying a *'What have you learned today?'* notice by the door of each classroom, and encouraging students to reflect on this question as they leave each lesson;

7   erecting a small black/white board in each classroom with the permanent heading, *'By the end of today's lesson, you will have learned...'* and encouraging teachers to complete the statement at the beginning of every lesson;

8   encouraging all teachers to attach a copy of their department's agreed goal (see Section Two, page 71) to their desks.

Involving the students

Any attempt to focus attention upon the learning process during lessons can be greatly assisted by involving students and their parents in the initiative.

● *Let students in on the secret of how they learn.* Teach them about the brain and how it operates, and provide them with a range of useful strategies for learning, such as mnemonics and review techniques. Give students plenty of opportunities in real learning situations to try out and develop these strategies.

● Teaching so-called 'study skills' in isolation, possibly as part of a PSE programme, is relatively ineffective. Students must be given *regular opportunities to develop effective learning techniques* across the curriculum, as part of their 'normal' lessons.

● *Consider running information evenings for parents to raise their awareness of how the brain learns* and the strategies that their children are being encouraged to adopt. Parental support and understanding of both how the students are working and what the school is trying to achieve can only be beneficial.

DO NOT DISTURB

LEARNING IN PROGRESS

Reviewing whole-school organization

Review the way in which the school is organized. Do whole-school policies, practices and structures help or hinder effective learning? In particular, consider:

1   *providing a breakfast bar facility* – the brain needs fuel, yet many students arrive at school without having had a proper breakfast;

2   *the lengths and frequency of breaks* – are students able to 'top up' the brain with food and water to keep it functioning effectively?

3   *providing drinking fountains* – are students able to get regular drinks?

4   *the lengths of your lessons* – lessons that are too long may have lots of 'middle' and lead to students becoming bored and losing concentration;

5   *how students end the day* – is there an opportunity for them to reflect upon what they have learned? Some schools end the day with a registration/tutor period, which provides an ideal opportunity for such reflection;

6   *how often lessons are disturbed* with messages and so on – lessons should be sacrosanct!

7   *Do you have a whole-school learning policy?* Is it displayed in the staffroom?

Overall strategy

The school needs to decide upon its strategy for developing the quality of teaching. Do you:

1   *Go for winners.* This often-used strategy involves identifying and working with staff who are most likely to be receptive to the messages that you wish to convey. The aim is to generate a momentum for the developments, which, if enough staff become involved, will eventually become irresistible. The caveat however is that the good teachers become better while those that would really benefit from developmental activities remain untouched by the process.

2   *Involve the whole staff simultaneously.* Whole-school priorities demand a whole-school response. No one feels isolated and neglected and no one feels singled out. Tackling an issue as a whole staff can lead to a feeling of ownership and team spirit. The danger here is that the initiative could be hijacked and ultimately derailed by a handful of hardened cynics who seemingly show little enthusiasm for any form of development.

3   *Develop a blitz approach.* Work intensively for short periods (a half-term, perhaps) with small groups of staff (between six and 12) or with each faculty in turn.

Don't try to slam your Learning Gap shut all at once; narrowing the gap, however slightly, is progress.

Warning!

- *Don't expect miracles.* Encouraging teachers, many of whom have been teaching for a great many years, is a major challenge. Even when teachers subscribe to the process, and are receptive to any new developments, they will not necessarily dramatically improve their practice overnight.

- *Be careful not to place teachers under undue pressure* and give the impression that they are required to make significant changes to their practice *immediately*. This will only increase the sense of unease and threat that many will naturally feel and is likely to be met with a highly defensive response.

- *Improving the quality of teaching in a school is a slow and continual process.* It requires commitment, energy and endless patience. It is well worth it, however, and when each new teacher commits themselves to reviewing and developing their practice, progress is being made and the school is improving.

Individual teachers should also be warned

Don't try to close your Learning Gap all at once, as this is likely to result in one or more of the following:

- *demotivation* – if teachers perceive the gap to be too large, or feel that they are being pressurised to close too much of it too quickly, they are unlikely to close it at all

- *disorientation of students* – trying to change teaching practice too much too soon will only confuse students and encourage them to be defensive; when this happens, strategies are unlikely to work and when they fail (sometimes with spectacular results) they are likely to be abandoned.

Having identified your Learning Gap, close it slowly, surely and systematically:

- Try closing the gap with one class or group at a time.

- Implement new strategies with younger students, as they are more likely to be receptive. Older students, who have been used to a particular style for a number of years, are often more resistant to change.

- Rather than trying a range of strategies with one group, consider implementing one new idea with each group that you teach.

- Don't expect new strategies to be instantly successful – it will take a little time for students to get used to a new way of working.

- Closing the Learning Gap does not have to involve a complete change in your current practice. Many of the points made in this book require only a subtle change in emphasis.

Unless teachers are clear about what they are looking for in the classroom, they will have difficulty seeing it.

OBSERVATION

Teaching is, or certainly can be, a lonely profession. Few teachers have substantial opportunities to observe colleagues in action or to be observed. How many lessons have you observed this year? Twenty? Ten? One?

Increasingly, however, schools are concluding that enabling teachers to visit each other in the classroom can have a beneficial effect upon classroom practice. It is a move that is to be applauded. However, I wish to begin this part of the book by highlighting a number of potential caveats.

One-off observations will have relatively little impact and will make virtually no difference to what is going on in the classroom. They will, however, be expensive and therefore serious questions are raised about whether an observation programme is cost-effective. I would suggest not only that increased opportunities for mutual observation can be effective, but also that the strategy is central to any drive to improve the quality of teaching. However, certain conditions must be met:

1   *Observations must be more than a one-off.* A single visit to another classroom makes little difference for either teacher. Teachers need to be given extensive opportunities to observe and to be observed. *It is all or nothing.*

2   *Observation is not an end in itself.* It is an activity that contributes to a wider process of reflection and professional development. We are not funding observation programmes to give people a break from the classroom, or so that they can watch their friend teach. We are creating opportunities for teachers to observe and to be observed to *help them become more effective teachers.*

3   *Unless teachers are clear about what they are looking for in the classroom, they will have difficulty seeing it.* I once talked to a colleague who was raving about a lesson he had just observed, describing it as *'fantastic'* and *'the best lesson he had ever seen'*. When I asked him why it was so good, he was unable to reply. The fact that he was unable to identify why it was such a good lesson made it extremely unlikely that he would be able to improve his practice as a result of the observation. Teachers must have gone through the process of 'setting the goal' (see page 73) prior to observing so that they are clear about what they are looking for.

4   *Teachers should receive 'observation training'.* Few teachers are trained in observation techniques, with most people developing their expertise through experience. While experience is vital, it can be helpful to kick-start the process with some training. It is important that people are trained *to observe* rather than be trained to *record their observations.* 'What' we are looking for is more important than 'how' we are going to write it down.

We are creating opportunities for observation in order to help teachers improve.

There is no single correct way to set up an observation programme or to carry out an observation. The important thing is that the school has considered and agreed upon certain key issues. The questions that need to be addressed are:

- Why?
- Who?
- What?
- When?
- How?

The rest of this part of the book considers each of these issues in turn, offering a personal view and highlighting some of the main factors that should be taken into account when observing lessons.

Why observe?

The objective of observation is to help teachers to improve and develop. If this is not your immediate answer to the question *'Why observe?'* then it is doubtful whether any observation programme will be worthwhile. If it is your answer, then it will significantly influence the way in which you respond to subsequent questions. Observation helps teachers improve, collectively and individually, by:

- keeping 'learning' high profile and focusing attention on classroom practice
- disseminating good practice
- encouraging reflection
- generating discussion about teaching and learning
- generating data to inform reflection and discussion
- providing teachers with a 'mirror' to enable them to get a clear picture of precisely what they do in the classroom
- helping to establish the Learning Gap
- identifying areas for development – helping to set the school improvement agenda.

Observation benefits both the observer and the observed. There will be occasions when a young teacher will benefit from observing a more experienced colleague in action; on other occasions, the main benefit will be to the teacher who has been observed and received feedback. However, to various degrees, both the observer and the observed will benefit from the observation process, often in an unplanned and unforeseen way.

EXAMPLE A: OBSERVATION TIME LINE

Teacher: **Date:**   **Group:**

Time (min)	Activity
0	
5	
10	
15	
20	
25	
30	
35	
40	
45	
50	
55	
60	

Who observes?

This is a key question, the answer being largely determined by your answer to the first question, *'Why observe?'* If you accept that classroom observation is essentially about helping teachers to improve, and not about accountability, the answer to *'Who observes?'* follows quite naturally.

For a key barrier (arguably *the* key barrier) to the development of teaching, and often a major factor in teachers' reluctance to embrace any professional development programme, is the feeling of threat and suspicion behind the motives. However sensitively it is carried out, any observation programme that relies solely on a line management or hierarchical model *will be perceived to be an accountability-driven strategy*, and will have limited impact. Many teachers will become defensive, even subconsciously, and the whole initiative will be carried out 'for the sake of it'.

Convincing teachers that observation can help them, and making the whole process non-threatening, is central to its success. Above all, teachers must trust both the person observing them and the wider motives behind such a programme.

Choose the observer carefully, for the observer is crucial to the success of the programme.

- The choice of observer should be non-threatening. Avoid reliance on hierarchical models. *Allow teachers to choose* their observer, or at least one of their observers. The whole process is significantly more effective if teachers are able to work with people with whom they feel comfortable.

- In many schools, the Head of Department is responsible for observing newly qualified teachers and younger members of staff. While this is important, it is equally important for young teachers to have extensive opportunities to observe more experienced colleagues. In many respects, these are the teachers who will most benefit from watching excellent practitioners at work.

- Don't forget to help your most experienced and effective teachers improve as well. It can be an effective way of reducing the sense of threat to allow young teachers - particularly if they are reticent about the whole process – to observe and feed back to more senior colleagues, before they themselves are observed. Experienced staff can set a positive example by demonstrating that feedback, even when it is constructively critical, is welcome if it helps the professional development process. It is a particularly powerful message when it is sent by the headteacher.

- Identify teachers who are particularly effective at aspects of classroom practice. For example, some are effective managers of group-work activities; others are particularly successful working with low achieving boys; while others have some interesting strategies for beginning lessons. Matching the needs of the observer with the particular expertise of the person being observed is important in maximizing the impact of observation and helping teachers close their personal Learning Gap.

Teacher

- Develop a comprehensive programme for each member of staff. Ensure that they have an opportunity to see a range of teachers in action, including:

  1 someone in the same department
  2 someone in another department
  3 another teacher teaching a group that they themselves teach
  4 someone with a very different 'Learning Gap profile,' that is someone with a very 'different' approach.

When to observe?

Teachers have to be comfortable with the timing of observation. Bear in mind that the whole process is designed to help teachers improve and that this is most likely to happen if they do not feel unduly threatened by the process. Consider the following:

- *Should teachers be observed with their 'best groups' or their 'worst groups' – should they be observed on a Tuesday morning or a Friday afternoon?*

  The initial aim must be to build up the teacher's trust and confidence in the entire programme. Therefore, start by allowing the teacher to choose the group; often they will choose a group they particularly enjoy teaching and with whom they experience no discipline problems. (It is unlikely that they will teach this group on Friday afternoon!)

  However, it is likely that these are the lessons in which the teacher's Learning Gap is at its smallest, and it is the groups the teacher finds most difficult that he or she would most benefit from help with. Our first aim must be to win the confidence of teachers and gain their commitment to the programme, but having done that, we must attempt to expand the observation programme to include lessons in which teachers experience less success.

- *Should observations be pre-arranged or should observers drop in unannounced?*

  Again, the key is to develop the trust of the people being observed and convince them that observation can help them develop their professional skills. The prospect of another teacher visiting a lesson unexpectedly is extremely unlikely to induce this response. However, knowing that a lesson is going to be observed is an artificial situation and can lead to teachers altering their approach for the occasion, however much they are encouraged not to.

  The aim is to try to help teachers become better teachers, rather than helping them to teach successful one-off lessons. Having started with a programme of pre-planned observations, it may be worthwhile considering whether to introduce some unannounced visits when the time is right.

Observation – what to look for:

- How do the students enter the classroom?
- Does the teacher greet the class?
- How does the teacher put children at their ease – with a smile?
- How does the teacher create a stress-free learning environment?
- How long after the bell does the class start learning?
- Does the teacher make use of the first ten minutes of the lesson?
- Are the objectives of the lesson clear? Are the students aware of them?
- How long does the introduction last?
- How long do other activities last?
- How many activities are included in the lesson?
- How much 'middle' is there in the lesson?
- How does the teacher cater for different learning styles?
- For what purpose does the teacher ask questions?
- To what extent do the questions help students to learn?
- Will the students remember the lesson? Is the experience dramatic or usual, or is it mundane?
- How engaged are the students in the lesson? To what extent are they required to 'do'? Is their 'contextual' memory activated?
- Are the students motivated?
- How are the activities developing understanding?
- Does the teacher recognize and respond to individual needs?
- How does the teacher know what has been understood?
- Is the lesson summarized and reinforced at the end?
- Are students encouraged to review their learning?
- How do students exit the classroom?

What have they learned?

Choose three words to describe the lesson. Your first reaction to this prompt is significant.

● *Do observations need to last the entire lesson?*

There is a danger that observations that last for only a part of a lesson are not afforded the same status as whole-lesson observations. Observers need to be prepared, and to give the lesson their undivided attention. This is far more likely to happen when there is a commitment to spend the entire lesson observing. It is too easy to be distracted and delayed by a telephone call or other 'urgent business' and dash into part of a lesson with other issues on your mind.

However, if the agreed focus of the lesson observation is the way in which the lesson starts and how effectively the teacher uses the first ten minutes of the period, then it may be appropriate for some observations to be confined to that part of the lesson. There must be a balance between what may be the ideal situation and the cost of any comprehensive observation programme.

What to observe?

Observers should be looking for the extent to which the lesson helps children to learn.

Questions that need to be addressed therefore include:

● What have they learned?

● How do you know?

● How is this activity helping them understand?

● How is this activity helping the teacher assess how much has been understood?

● How much of the lesson is likely to be remembered?

In general terms, observers should be looking for anything – atmosphere, strategies and activities – that will help students to learn, and anything that will limit or even prevent learning. It is therefore *important that the observer has a clear understanding of the learning process* and the relationship between learning, understanding and memory, discussed on pages 61–63.

This is why any observation programme *should be preceded by careful consideration about precisely what it is we are trying to do in the classroom*, in which both parties should have been involved. Having established the goal in this way – having considered the *'how'* as well as the *'what'* (see page 77) – both teachers should know the basis on which the observation is taking place.

It is equally important to be clear about what we are not looking for; we are *not* looking for styles, strategies or classroom organization that we ourselves employ or prefer. For example, although we may not ourselves encourage children to work in groups (our feelings may be even stronger than that), we must avoid the temptation to spend the lesson reflecting that *'I wouldn't have done it this way'*. The point is to focus upon learning, and to observe the lesson by looking for the ways in which the selected activities help or hinder learning.

EXAMPLE C: OBSERVATION TALLY CHART

Teacher talking	~~IIII~~ ~~IIII~~ ~~IIII~~ IIII
Pupil talking	IIII
Question and answers	~~IIII~~ III
Group-work/activity	
Written work	II
Reading	I
Taking notes	
Paired work	

Lesson observations will be more effective if they concentrate upon a specific aspect of the lesson and have an agreed focus. The focus will be informed by the department's agreed goal (see page 71) and by the individual teacher's perceived Learning Gap. It is finalized by negotiation.

For example, the observer might focus attention upon:

- the quality of questioning
- the lengths of activities
- the beginning of the lesson
- the extent to which the activities develop understanding
- one student.

Initially, teachers may feel more comfortable with a focus for the observation that they feel is a relative strength of their classroom practice. This will hopefully enable the observer to give some positive feedback, reduce any feelings of threat and help develop the relationship between the observer and the observed.

We must keep in mind, however, that the purpose of observation is to help teachers improve by helping them both identify and close their personal Learning Gap. Eventually, therefore, the focus of the observation must switch to the aspects of teaching that an individual may consider relatively weak.

This is a critical time, for if teachers becomes demotivated they will become defensive and may well opt out of the process, even subconsciously, altogether. When this happens, to any significant degree, any further developments in practice are extremely unlikely. *Morale must be maintained at all costs!* This can be achieved, even when the process begins to move into potentially sensitive areas, by simultaneously looking at two aspects of the lesson, a perceived strength and an issue that the teacher is less confident about.

How to observe?

The first challenge for the school is to provide sufficient time to allow a comprehensive observation programme to go ahead. Some suggestions of how to create time for such an initiative are given on pages 137–141. If you cannot answer the question 'how can this be funded?' then *stop reading here.*

The following three issues need to be considered and decided upon:

1   What am I looking for? (See page 157.)
2   How shall I record my observations?
3   How is the observation going to be organized?

Recording observations
There is no single correct way to record an observation. Much depends on personal preferences, which range from scribbling a few notes on the back of an envelope, to conscientiously filling in detailed pro formas.

EXAMPLE D: OBSERVATION – IMPACT ON LEARNING

Teacher: William   Date: 1066   Group: 7K

Time (min)		Activity	Impact on learning (0–5 scale)
0		Students enter room etc.	0
5	8	Lesson begins. Recap on last lesson. A few questions (closed) directed at 4 students.	2
10		Some students still settling.	
	12	Teacher explains what Magna Carta was. KEY POINT.	3/2
15			
20	21	Students read from book (few appear to be reading).	1 (variable)
25		Students copy paragraph from text book (one or two have lost concentration).	1
30			
35	37	As students finish, they are directed to questions at the end of text (James is looking out of window).	2
40		Claire says 'I don't get number one' (check reading age). Teacher says 'The answer is in the text'. (Reading age 13)	2
45		Gareth finished after 48 mins.	2
50		Most finished after 51–53 mins.	1
55	57	Homework – complete additional activities.	0
60			

There is a fine balance between the need to record your observations and generate data for subsequent feedback and discussion, and concentrating on the lesson rather than your notes. It is difficult to record and observe at the same time. Many people fall into the trap of *over-recording*.

Observations fall into three broad categories, which demand slightly different approaches to recording:

1 *When the observer is looking to gain an overall impression of the lesson, there is no need to take detailed notes.* By limiting notes to a few jottings on a blank piece of paper, attention can be focused firmly on the lesson itself. Identify and make notes of anything that you feel is helping students to learn and anything that may be limiting their learning.

   At the end of the observation write down three words that sum up the lesson that you have just witnessed; your first thoughts will be significant.

2 *More detailed notes are required when the purpose of the observation is to provide a factual feedback to the teacher.* These are the observations that essentially 'hold up a mirror' so that teachers can 'see' themselves in action. The key here is to record what happened rather than to write judgements about how effective the lesson was. For example, record that the introduction lasted 19 minutes, or that, of the 17 questions asked, 12 were asked of boys.

   Time lines and simple pro formas are useful in these instances (such as Example A, page 152). It is also helpful to use a stopwatch, in order to report back when things happened.

3 *Many observations will concentrate on particular aspects of the lesson and the learning process* and this specific focus will largely determine the style of recording that is required. Example B (page 154) is an example of a pro forma that is ideal for recording student participation during a question and answer session. Each time a particular student answers a question, they are 'circled'. There are many variations on this theme – you could use a different colour if the student volunteers to answer, as opposed to being asked directly, or use different colours to denote open and closed questions.

Observations should not be limited to what is seen. Isolate the relevant sense in order to enhance it. For example, if you are interested in the quality of questioning, listen to the lesson rather than watching it. Sit facing the wall and pay particular attention to the questions that are asked and how they are delivered. Are they open or closed? Do they challenge students to think and help them learn? Do they put students under undue pressure? How does the teacher deal with students who do not respond when asked a question?

If there is time, every question could be written down in order for the teacher to reflect on his or her use of questioning at a later date. Alternatively, record open and closed questions as 'O' and 'C', or give each question a rating between 0 and 5 depending on the extent to which it helps the students learn. Is there any pattern to the questioning? For example, does the lesson start with a flurry of closed questions?

EXAMPLE E: OBSERVATION – IMPACT ON LEARNING (POSITIVE / NEGATIVE)

Teacher: Subject: Class:

Time (mins)	Contributes to learning	Limits learning
0	Teacher greets group at door with smile. Relaxed.	
5	Clear objectives.	
10		Succession of closed questions. No thought required.
15	Paired work – identify 6 keywords from text.	
20	Classwork – sharing of words.	Drags on too long – students losing concentration.
25		
30	2 or 3 benefit from teacher explanation.	Teacher explanation, but most have lost concentration (no state break.
35		
40	Students collect Atlases. Stretch legs – state break.	
45	Use Atlases to describe (what) and explain (why).	
50		
55		Rushed ending. No consolidation/review. Homework hurriedly given out.
60		

Closing the Learning Gap

Pro formas can be particularly useful when the observer is relatively inexperienced as they help to provide a focus for the observation. They are most useful when they have been designed by the observer, and have *taken into account the purpose of the lesson* and their personal preferences. Indeed, the very process of thinking about and designing the form is a worthwhile exercise and helps the observer consider precisely why they are visiting a particular lesson and specifically what they are looking for.

Pro formas for recording lesson observations need to include three essential pieces of information:

1   what happened

2   when it happened

3   the extent to which it contributed to or limited learning.

A number of suggested recording sheets are included in these pages: Examples A, B and C are designed to record what happened and when. They are appropriate when feedback is at stages one and two (see page 171), that is *before* judgements are offered.

Example A (page 152)   This is a simple time line with space for the observer to note down what is happening at various stages of the lesson.

Example B (page 154)   This is a plan of the classroom – each student is marked as an 'X' (an alternative to represent boys and girls as 'B' and 'G'). The student is ringed every time he or she answers a question or contributes to the lesson. By using different colours, it is possible to distinguish between answers that were volunteered and answers to questions that were directed to the student. Colour can also be used to record whether questions were open or closed. In this example, a small number of students – one in particular – have dominated the lesson, with the teacher seemingly favouring the side of the classroom to his or her left.

Example C (page 158)   This is a tally chart. Every minute (approximately) the observer records what is happening. This is an effective way of generating data to complete the scatter graph activity on pages 84–85.

Examples D, E, F and G also enable the observer to record what is happening and when, but offer in addition the opportunity to record judgements about the *impact* each activity is having upon learning. They are particularly appropriate when the feedback has progressed beyond stage two (see page 171).

Example D (page 160)   This is an enhanced time line. It simply allows the observer to grade each activity on a 0–5 scale for the contribution it makes to learning. Although this is inevitably a subjective exercise, it does give a rough indication of the observer's feelings during the lesson. (Note the 'key learning point' coming after 12 minutes in this lesson.)

Example E (page 162)   This sheet requires less information about *what* is happening to be recorded but instead requires the observer to record judgements about the impact the activities are having upon learning.

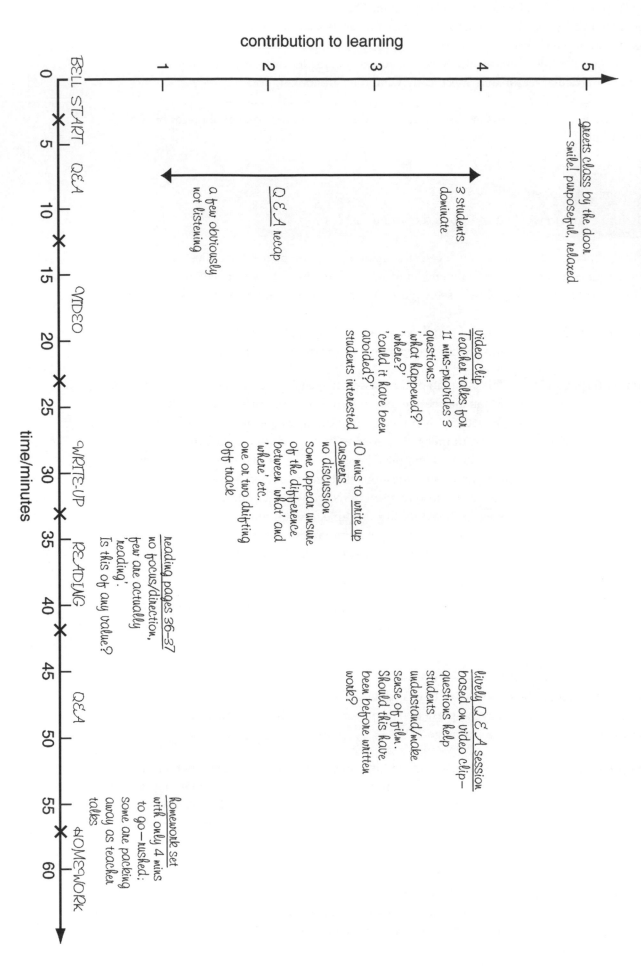

contribution to learning

5

4

3

2

1

0   5   10   15   20   25   30   35   40   45   50   55   60

time/minutes

BELL START   Q&A   VIDEO   WRITE-UP   READING   Q&A   HOMEWORK

greets class by the door
— smile! purposeful, relaxed

3 students
dominate

_Q & A_ recap

a few obviously
not listening

video clip
Teacher talks for
11 mins-provides 3
questions:
'what happened?'
'where?'
'could it have been
avoided?'
students interested

10 mins to _write up_
answers
no discussion
Some appear unsure
of the difference
between 'what' and
'where' etc.
one or two drifting
off track

reading pages 36-37
no focus/direction,
few are actually
'reading'.
Is this of any value?

lively Q & A session
based on video clip-
questions help
students
understand/make
sense of film.
Should this have
been before written
work?

homework set
with only 4 mins
to go—rushed;
Some are packing
away as teacher
talks

Example F (page 164)   This sheet combines the key features of a line graph with a
time line. There is an opportunity to record *what* is happening,
when it happens and the *impact* each event has upon learning.
It can be compiled during the lesson or completed afterwards
by plotting information from a sheet such as Example D on to
the graph axes. This highly visual representation makes it
easier for many people to detect patterns and can considerably
strengthen the message. In this example, there appears to be a
dip between 35 and 50 minutes. If this pattern were to be
repeated on several occasions, a definite Learning Gap would
emerge. It can be of interest to superimpose this information
on the BEM graph on page 36.

Example G (page 166)   This sheet is appropriate if the focus of the observation is the
way in which students with different learning styles are
catered for.

Warning

Great care should be taken when interpreting sheets such as these, once completed. For
example, a three-minute period in which no learning is apparently taking place may
actually be a planned and necessary 'state break' that will significantly enhance learning
during the remainder of the lesson. Sheets like these are useful as a guide and to provide
a pattern to the lesson; they must, however, be treated with care.

Organizing observations

There is no 'correct' way to organize an observation; however, there are two golden
rules:

1   There should be *no surprises!* All procedures should be agreed in advance.

2   The observer should be as *unobtrusive* as possible.

It is therefore important that the organization is discussed and agreed prior to the
observation taking place. The following is a checklist of considerations that need to be
addressed before you observe a lesson:

1   *What, if anything, do you tell the students?* If observation is a normal everyday
occurrence, it may not be necessary to say anything. A brief word, however, may
reassure them that there is nothing to worry about and enable the lesson to proceed
as normally as possible.

2   *Does the observer arrive before, with, or after the students?* My preference is to arrive,
whenever possible, before the students. Watching a group arrive can give important
clues about their expectations and feelings about the particular lesson.

EXAMPLE G: **OBSERVATION – LEARNING STYLES**

Teacher:	Subject:	Class:
Visual	Auditory	Kinesthetic

0

5

10

15

20

25

30

35

40

45

50

55

60

3   *Where will the observer sit?* This will, in part, depend upon the focus of the observation. The key is to be unobtrusive and, to this end, it is important to determine where the observer will sit in advance – it can be most off-putting for another teacher to be wandering around the room looking for a chair while you are trying to start the lesson.

Do not assume that the observer must sit at the back, as this position prevents observation of the students' reactions to various parts of the lesson. Unless the focus of the lesson demands otherwise, I favour a side view.

4   *Will the observer write notes during the lesson?* Almost certainly the answer to this will be 'yes'. It is, however, worth agreeing this beforehand so that when the pen and notepad appear, the teacher is not taken by surprise.

5   *When will the observer receive a copy of the resources that are to be used?* There is nothing worse than trying to observe a lesson without having a copy of the worksheet or textbook in front of you. It doesn't matter when you get it, simply that you do.

6   *Put the lesson in context* prior to the observation. It is very helpful if the observer is aware of:

● what happened last lesson

● how the lesson will be followed up

● relevant information about the group – for example, whether there are any students who are on the Special Needs Register.

The purpose of feeding back is to help teachers improve.

FEEDBACK

Feedback is an essential, yet often neglected, stage in the improvement process. Increasingly, schools are creating opportunities for teachers to observe colleagues in action, but these opportunities are not always accompanied with time to discuss the lesson afterwards. This is short sighted, as *observation without feedback will have relatively little impact on classroom performance.*

It is also ironic that so few teachers have received any form of training in the business of feedback. Few have been trained how to *give* feedback, and even fewer trained in how to *receive* it.

Although feeding back and discussing a lesson after it has been observed significantly increases the time demand of any teacher observation programme, it is an investment well worth making. Feedback may require around twice the time of observation alone, but will have more than double the impact.

There is no single correct way of feeding back, although there are some general principles that should be observed. The most important of these is that everyone involved in the programme should have considered the key issues and addressed the basic questions *'why?'*, *'how?'*, *'what?'*, *'where?'* and *'when?'* prior to the observation taking place.

Why feed back?

Quite simply, the *purpose of feeding back is to help teachers improve*. It is an answer that has a considerable bearing upon subsequent questions.

Releasing a teacher to observe a colleague teach involves a financial cost and an opportunity cost – what else could they have been doing with that time? These are costs that can only be justified if teachers are going to improve as result of the experience.

Teachers will not improve if they feel they are being unfairly criticized. Worse still, they will not even listen. When people feel they are being attacked, their natural response is to defend and they will adopt a defensive mode as soon as they perceive an attack is being launched, however unjustified this view may be.

In order for teachers to improve, their morale must be maintained and the motivation to develop their practice left firmly intact. Above all their self-respect and sense of professional and personal worth must remain unblemished; when hope is lost, all is lost and the process is as good as over.

The four-stage approach to feedback:

1 giving reassurance

2 providing information

3 evaluating

4 life after feedback.

How to feed back?

Consider a four-stage approach to feeding back. Not all stages will be reached on every occasion; indeed, you may need to stay in stage 1 for some considerable time before moving on. Similarly, it may be appropriate to skip a stage or two if you have been working with a colleague for some time and a genuine rapport has developed.

The four stages are:

Stage 1	giving reassurance
Stage 2	providing information – 'hold up a mirror'
Stage 3	evaluating
Stage 4	life after feedback.

Stage 1 – giving reassurance

Arguably, this is the most important stage of the feedback process because if the person feeding back is unable to reassure his or her colleague, the process will never move through the remaining phases.

By opening their classroom doors to a colleague teachers place themselves in a potentially vulnerable position. As the feedback begins they will naturally be anxious and looking for the slightest sign that their colleague has found fault in the lesson they have just taught. While this attitude is perfectly understandable, it is also a state of mind that will prevent them from hearing, and certainly from digesting, anything that the observer has to say.

It is a state that needs to be broken before any worthwhile and constructive feedback is given, and which dictates that the primary goal of anyone debriefing a colleague is to *win his or her trust, confidence and respect*. This may take time and will probably not be achieved during the first observation session. It cannot be rushed or overlooked and it must be achieved, however long it takes, before moving on to the next stage.

Teachers will not develop their practice simply by being observed, nor will they improve just because someone has told them what they are doing 'wrong'. Improvement requires an internal process; practice will only develop when the individual identifies areas of relative weakness and accepts the need to improve. The process of observation and feedback is simply a catalyst to this process.

Before the whole process can begin in earnest, however, teachers have to be convinced that the observer is on their side and it is only when they accept that they are not being attacked that they will stop defending. Start any feedback by telling the teacher how much you enjoyed the lesson and *highlight the aspects of their performance that were particularly strong*. Do this for as long as it takes to win the confidence of the teacher, be it minutes or weeks, before you move on. Above all, smile!

'Your introduction lasted **27 minutes.**'

'You asked **21** questions – **15** to boys and six to girls.'

'The first pupil finished the activity after seven minutes.'

Closing the Learning Gap

Stage 2 – providing information

Stage 2 involves providing the teacher with factual information about the lesson that has just been observed. In this stage, the role of the observer is to 'hold up a mirror' so that the teacher can see exactly what happened during the lesson and when. There is no need at this stage to offer any judgement, explicit or otherwise – only data. By avoiding making judgements, particularly negative ones, the process of reassurance that was begun in stage one is developed further.

The information provided during the feedback fuels and informs the self-reflection process that the teacher has almost certainly begun. When teachers have been observed and know they are going to receive feedback they often will go over the lesson in their own minds, which they would almost certainly *not* do if there had not been an observer present.

Often, information of the sort suggested opposite is all that is required for the improvement process to begin. Few teachers *plan* to talk for 27 minutes at the beginning of the lesson, knowing that the concentration of their students will begin to drift after around 15 minutes. Many teachers are unaware that they tend to talk too much at the beginning of the lesson, with the vast majority significantly underestimating how long they have talked for. Similarly, most teachers believe that they have asked approximately the same number of questions to boys and girls – certainly, few would consciously discriminate in this way – and often greet the actual figures with a sense of disbelief.

It is often unnecessary to proceed beyond the stage of information provision; few teachers need to be told that 27-minute introductions are too long or that the way forward for them is to limit the amount of time that they talk for to around ten minutes. By 'holding up a mirror', the observer provides teachers with a different view of their lessons, enabling them to see clearly what they are doing and to identify areas in which they could improve their practice.

Stage 3 – evaluating

This is a stage that can only be reached after stages 1 and 2 have been successfully negotiated and a feeling of mutual trust has been developed. Even when such a relationship has been established, however, it is important that any judgements that are offered during a feedback session are:

1 *made sensitively* – a relationship that has been nurtured over many weeks can be destroyed by an insensitive remark, however well intentioned.

2 *are firmly based in evidence* – 'I think you talked too much', is an opinion; 'Your introduction lasted for 27 minutes. Judging by the way in which you had to ask Jonathon to stop looking out of the window and reprimand Sam and Alison for fidgeting, I think that was maybe a little too long', is a judgement based upon evidence.

Observation and feedback is like holding up a mirror to enable colleagues to see themselves in action.

3   *relate to how effectively the lesson helped the students learn* – the key question that needs to be addressed is 'what did they learn?' and only judgements (based upon evidence) that attempt to provide an answer are valid; for example, 'I'm not sure how much they understood. I asked three pupils about the difference between an atom and an element, and none of them could answer'. Feedback is not an opportunity for observers to claim, 'well, I wouldn't have done it that way', or 'there wasn't much groupwork', simply because they prefer to work in a different manner, unless the style adopted has had a direct bearing upon the amount that has been understood and learned.

4   *limited to identification of only one area for development* – however sensitively an area for improvement is wrapped up, it is still, by implication at least, a negative comment and has the power to demoralize, particularly if the criticism is accepted. Teachers who hear that they have four, five or more aspects of their performance that require attention, even when positive comments outweigh negative feedback by 10:1, are likely to be so dispirited that none of the issues will be addressed. Teachers must be allowed to address areas of their performance that need attention in isolation.

This is the stage at which the implications of the factual information fed back during stage 2 are discussed and considered. It is not the moment for observers to tell their colleagues what they have done wrong, whatever the relative experience of the two.

The key for the person offering the judgement is to ensure that the teacher who has been observed accepts at least the need to reflect on the issue that has been raised, even if they do not immediately agree with the view. *Even when judgements are not accepted, they have the capacity to generate substantial professional debate and stimulate thought and discussion* that will continue, for both parties, long after the formal feedback session has ended. When conducted in a sensitive and stimulating manner, they can develop a self-reflection momentum that can often prove irresistible.

It can be profitable at this stage to *provide teachers who have been observed with the first opportunity to judge their own lessons* and to draw initial conclusions about the information provided during stage 2. This allows the discussion to begin without jeopardizing the relationship that has been so painstakingly developed in the preceding weeks. The use of prompt questions can be effective in 'getting the ball rolling'.

For example:

- What did you think of the lesson?
- Would you do anything different next time? If so, what? Why?
- What aspects of the lesson were you particularly pleased with?
- Were there any aspects of the lesson that you were less pleased with?
- What would be an alternative way of delivering that lesson? How was the way you chose more effective?

The answers to these questions can often open the discussion and provide an opportunity to reply; for example, 'I imagine that you've reached that conclusion because no one was able to answer your question at the end.' It is far easier to offer a judgement and highlight the evidence for it if the teacher has already made that judgement himself or herself.

Feeding back is about helping the teacher to identify the way forward.

Closing the Learning Gap

Stage 4 – life after feedback

Feeding back is about helping teachers to identify the way forward for them. They must leave the feedback session both *wanting* to develop their practice – which is largely dependent upon how sensitively the feedback has been provided – and with a clear *understanding of what to do next.*

In many cases, the way forward is self-evident. For example, teachers who have identified that their particular Learning Gap is the result of them talking too much, particularly at the beginning of the lesson, know that they must make a conscious effort to limit the length of their introductions.

However, while it is often relatively straightforward to identify areas of classroom practice that could be developed, it is sometimes less easy to provide 'quick fix' solutions. In these instances, a valuable outcome of observation and feedback is to arrange for the teacher concerned to be able to observe and talk to a member of staff who is particularly proficient in the aspect of teaching that has been agreed as an area for development. There is a vast range of expertise within any school; the trick is to *identify which teacher is best able to help another individual close his or her Learning Gap.*

Feedback is not a one-off event; it is part of a continual process of review and development. We must therefore ensure that teachers emerge from the experience with both a clear understanding of their personal Learning Gap and a concrete strategy to enable them to close it.

Possible information to provide during feedback:

- how long after the bell that learning started

- what the teacher said first

- what happened

- when things happened

- how long the introduction lasted

- how many questions were asked

- how many questions were directed to boys/girls

- the reading age of the resources

- evidence that students were losing concentration

- how long it took for the first/last student to finish a task

- evidence that the students understood what was required of them (what they had to do)

- evidence that the students understood the content

- the timing of the key learning point.

What to feed back?

The purpose of providing feedback is to help teachers improve, so it must therefore provide any information that assists in that process. However, the nature of the information and amount of detail that is provided will largely depend upon which of the four stages of feedback we are in and the purpose of the observation.

As a general rule of thumb, we need to *feed back anything about the lesson that had an impact upon learning*, from body language to tasks, from furniture layout to resources. More specifically, the feedback should identify any aspect of the lesson that contributed to, limited or even prevented learning. This type of feedback tends to occur early in the observation process and provides a broad range of 'what happened and when' information.

As the programme progresses and the observations develop a much sharper and specific focus, so the range of information fed back will narrow and, simultaneously, the amount of detail fed back will increase. For example, if the focus of the observation was the quality of the questioning, then the bulk of information provided afterwards should relate to the questions that had been asked. Observations are at their most effective when the observer is looking for specific factors in order to provide detailed and specific feedback.

When to feed back?

Feedback should be given close enough after the lesson for the key issues to be firmly in the minds of the observer and observed and every attempt should be made to enable the discussion to take place *on the same day as the lesson occurred*. Teachers feel anxious enough after they have allowed a colleague to watch them teach without having to drive home wondering what they thought of it.

There is, however, a case to be made for avoiding arranging a feedback meeting for immediately after the lesson. Both teachers benefit from a little time to catch their metaphorical breath and organize their thoughts before entering into detailed discussion.

The teacher who has just taught the lesson benefits from a short delay by having a chance to shed the emotion, adrenaline and anxiety, that will prevent him or her from hearing clearly the message of the feedback. The observer benefits in a slightly different way; he or she is able to reflect on what has just been seen and consider the most sensitive and effective way to debrief the teacher.

There is no 'correct' time to feed back, and much depends upon the preferences of the teachers directly involved. However, there is a powerful argument to suggest that the prime time to feed back after a lesson observation is later on the same day.

Feedback is not a one-off event; it is part of a continual process of review and development.

Where to feed back?

In considering a suitable venue for a feedback session, the key consideration must be to put both teachers – but particularly the teacher who has been observed – at ease. It is therefore important that:

● *a venue is found where the meeting will be undisturbed* – it is helpful to put an appropriate notice on the door and to unplug the telephone;

● *the meeting does not take place in a line managers office* – holding a feedback session in the Head of Department's or Deputy Head's office sends out a message of 'accountability' and will immediately create a sense of threat; if possible, select a 'neutral' venue;

● *the observer does not adopt the 'power position'* – it is impossible to create the feeling of mutual trust and respect when looking up to the person feeding back to you with the sun shining directly into your eyes; the observer and the observed are equal partners in this process and the furniture and their respective positions should reflect this.

■ **What three things have you found most interesting about this book?**

___

■ **What three things will you do differently from now on?**

___

■ **What three things do you want to find out more about?**

___

SUGGESTED READING

Lessons are for Learning, Mike Hughes (Network Educational Press, 1997)
ISBN 1 85539 038 8.

Strategies for Closing the Learning Gap, Mike Hughes with Andy Vass (Network Educational Press, 2001)
ISBN 1 85539 075 2.

Tweak to Transform, Mike Hughes with David Potter (Network Educational Press, 2002)
ISBN 1 85539 140 6.

Accelerated Learning in Practice, Alistair Smith (Network Educational Press, 1998)
ISBN 1 85539 048 5.

The Learning Revolution, G Dryden and J Voss (Network Educational Press, 2001)
ISBN 1 85539 085 X.

The Learning Brain, Eric Jensen (Turning Point Publishing USA, 1994)
ISBN 0 9637832 3 X.

Super Teaching, Eric Jensen (Turning Point Publishing USA, 1995)
ISBN 0 9637832 0 3.

Completing the Puzzle, Eric Jensen (The Brain Store Inc, 1996)
ISBN 0 9637832 5 4.

Use Your Memory, Tony Buzan (BBC Books, 1986)
ISBN 0563 37102 1.

Accelerated Learning, Colin Rose (Accelerated Learning Systems Ltd, 1985)
ISBN 0 905553 128.

INDEX

Titles from Network Educational Press

THE SCHOOL EFFECTIVENESS SERIES

Book 1: *Accelerated Learning in the Classroom* by Alistair Smith
Book 2: *Effective Learning Activities* by Chris Dickinson
Book 3: *Effective Heads of Department* by Phil Jones & Nick Sparks
Book 4: *Lessons are for Learning* by Mike Hughes
Book 5: *Effective Learning in Science* by Keith Bishop & Paul Denley
Book 6: *Raising Boys' Achievement* by Jon Pickering
Book 7: *Effective Provision for Able & Talented Children* by Barry Teare
Book 8: *Effective Careers Education & Guidance* by Andrew Edwards & Anthony Barnes
Book 9: *Best behaviour and Best behaviour FIRST AID* by Peter Relf, Rod Hirst, Jan Richardson & Georgina Youdell
   Best behaviour FIRST AID also available separately
Book 10: *The Effective School Governor* by David Marriott (including audio tape)
Book 11: *Improving Personal Effectiveness for Managers in Schools* by James Johnston
Book 12: *Making Pupil Data Powerful* by Maggie Pringle & Tony Cobb
Book 13: *Closing the Learning Gap* by Mike Hughes
Book 14: *Getting Started* by Henry Liebling
Book 15: *Leading the Learning School* by Colin Weatherley
Book 16: *Adventures in Learning* by Mike Tilling
Book 17: *Strategies for Closing the Learning Gap* by Mike Hughes with Andy Vass
Book 18: *Classroom Management* by Philip Waterhouse & Chris Dickinson
Book 19: *Effective Teachers* by Tony Swainston
Book 20: *Transforming Teaching & Learning* by Colin Weatherley with Bruce Bonney, John Kerr & Jo Morrison
Book 21: *Effective Teachers in Primary Schools* by Tony Swainston

ACCELERATED LEARNING SERIES   General Editor: **Alistair Smith**

Accelerated Learning in Practice by Alistair Smith
The ALPS Approach: Accelerated Learning in Primary Schools
by Alistair Smith & Nicola Call
MapWise by Oliver Caviglioli & Ian Harris
The ALPS Approach Resource Book by Alistair Smith & Nicola Call
Creating an Accelerated Learning School by Mark Lovatt & Derek Wise
ALPS StoryMaker by Stephen Bowkett
Thinking for Learning by Mel Rockett & Simon Percival
Reaching out to all learners by Cheshire LEA
Leading Learning by Alistair Smith
Bright Sparks by Alistair Smith
More Bright Sparks by Alistair Smith
Move It by Alistair Smith

EDUCATION PERSONNEL MANAGEMENT SERIES

*The Well Teacher – management strategies for beating stress, promoting staff health &
reducing absence* by Maureen Cooper
Managing Challenging People – dealing with staff conduct by Maureen Cooper & Bev Curtis
Managing Poor Performance – handling staff capability issues
by Maureen Cooper & Bev Curtis
*Managing Allegations Against Staff – personnel and child protection issues
in schools* by Maureen Cooper & Bev Curtis
Managing Recruitment and Selection – appointing the best staff
by Maureen Cooper & Bev Curtis
Managing Redundancies – dealing with reduction and reorganisation of staff
by Maureen Cooper & Bev Curtis
Paying Staff in Schools – performance management and pay in schools
by Bev Curtis

VISIONS OF EDUCATION SERIES

The Power of Diversity by Barbara Prashnig
The Unfinished Revolution by John Abbott & Terry Ryan
The Learning Revolution by Gordon Dryden & Jeannette Vos
Wise Up by Guy Claxton

ABLE & TALENTED CHILDREN COLLECTION

Effective Resources for Able and Talented Children by Barry Teare
More Effective Resources for Able and Talented Children by Barry Teare
Challenging Resources for Able and Talented Children by Barry Teare

MODEL LEARNING

Thinking Skills & Eye Q by Oliver Caviglioli, Ian Harris & Bill Tindall
Think it–Map it! by Ian Harris & Oliver Caviglioli

OTHER TITLES FROM NEP

The Thinking Child by Nicola Call with Sally Featherstone
StoryMaker Catch Pack by Stephen Bowkett
Becoming Emotionally Intelligent by Catherine Corrie
That's Science! by Tim Harding
The Brain's Behind It by Alistair Smith
Help Your Child To Succeed by Bill Lucas & Alistair Smith
Tweak to Transform by Mike Hughes
Brain Friendly Revision by UFA National Team
Numeracy Activities Key Stage 2 by Afzal Ahmed & Honor Williams
Numeracy Activities Key Stage 3 by Afzal Ahmed, Honor Williams & George Wickham
Teaching Pupils How to Learn by Bill Lucas, Toby Greany, Jill Rodd & Ray Wicks
Creating a Learning to Learn School by Toby Greany & Jill Rodd
Basics for School Governors by Joan Sallis
Imagine That... by Stephen Bowkett
Self-Intelligence by Stephen Bowkett
Class Talk by Rosemary Sage
Lend Us Your Ears by Rosemary Sage

For more information and ordering details, please consult our website
www.networkpress.co.uk

UNIVERSITY OF WALES, NEWPORT
LIBRARY AND INFORMATION SERVICES CAERLEON